Essential Worship

Drawing Closer To God

The Book:

Worship is an act, as in taking communion or falling to one's knees in prayer. It's an attitude, as when we are filled by singing or hearing a hymn. It is a recognition of both the greatness of God above us and the closeness of God to us. However, worship can go further than that, attempting to recover at least some part of our oneness with God that we lost at the gates of Eden. In Essential Worship, we consider three things that separate us from God and four steps we can take to draw closer.

I believe that through our best worship, when our worship is neither an act nor an attitude but is at our very essence, we can come very close to Essential Worship.

The Author:

In his sixty-plus-year career, Chuck Holmes has written all sorts of things: television scripts, industrial shows, speeches, training, a novel, short stories, and menu blurbs, just to name a few, but the experience that has the greatest relevance to this book is his forty years as a Sunday School teacher. He draws on that experience, plus decades of Bible study to examine how we might better approach God in our worship.

Essential Worship

Drawing Closer To God

by

Chuck Holmes

CS/Books Tucker, GA

Published by: CS/Books, Tucker, GA

Library of Congress Cataloging-in-Publications data is availableon request.

ISBN-13: 979-8-218-96613-3

First Edition, 2023

This book is dedicated to
all of the pastors who
have guided my journey
for these eighty-plus years,
especially Reverend Thurmond Stone,
Reverend H. O. Lanning, Pastor Hoffman Harris,
Dr. John Wyatt, and Dr. Don Pratt.
These have played important parts
in special times in my life.
I'm grateful to all of them.

Other books by Chuck Holmes

The Sing
A Novel

More Than Just Cellular
& Other Musings on Life, Past, Present, and Eternal

The World Beyond the Window
& Other Stories

Small Stories
With Michael Nelson

These books are available online at Amazon, Barnes & Noble and chuckholes.org and may be ordered through independent book stores. Books ordered from the author's website will be signed on request.

A study guide for individual and group study of Essential Worship is available as a PDF download from chuckholmes.org.

Chuck Holmes may be contacted at through his website.

Table of Contents

Introduction

This is, as I'm sure you'll discover for yourself, not a scholarly book. It does have footnotes, but they are simply to give credit where credit is due; most of what I know I learned from someone else. However, beyond that, this is a very personal book. It began as an effort to put into some sort of coherent form answers to questions that have been rolling around in my head for my eighty-plus years. In teaching Sunday School for most of my adult life, I've encountered any number of answers in the Sunday School quarterly that struck me as being too easy or too pat to be satisfying. As a husband, a parent, and a writer, I lived in worlds of ambiguity and didn't usually encounter such clearly drawn solutions in my own life. I wondered how the people in our Bible studies managed it.

I came to the conclusion that much of the material in the Teacher's Quarterly was designed not so much to teach the Bible as to teach the lesson that the writers and editors of the lesson series wanted to be taught. Consequently, those quarrelsome details that blurred the edges of Sunday's takeaway were simply eliminated.

Generally, I taught the lesson more or less as written, believing—as did the people who wrote it—that a good Sunday School lesson should have something the student can use rather than just think about. Occasionally, I would range afield and get into something that would make the class members reassess what they had been thinking.

For instance, why was Solomon, who had a thousand wives and 300 concubines, or Abraham, who had a child by Hagar, not committing adultery, and David, who pursued Bathsheba, was? Or, to put it more starkly, how is a married man having sex outside of marriage, not adultery? I explained that the commandment regarding adultery isn't really about sex but about property. I also explained that this was not an explanation that I would try to support in modern times.

Then some things were interesting to me but not necessarily pertinent to a particular Sunday School lesson, such as the story of Judah and Tamar in Genesis 38. Over the years, every time we studied the Book of Genesis, the Bible would interrupt our study of Joseph with what seemed to be an unrelated segment of a soap opera. In a single chapter, two sons died, a father-in-law was seduced, and twins were born. Then it was over, and we returned to the Joseph saga, already in progress. Since I believe that everything in the Bible is put there for a purpose, I've kept returning to the question: Why Judah and Tamar? It's true that Judah is related to Joseph (both in terms of the story and the family) and that one of the children resulting from Judah and Tamar's brief fling is counted as an ancestor of David and of Jesus. However, from a writer's point of view, it's a strange place to drop the story.

The Bible is full of interesting questions, and seeking answers to them is both challenging and fun. However, somewhere in the thinking about this book, the questions I started to answer began to coalesce around a single, larger, and what appears a much more profound one: How do we properly respond to God? More specifically, how do we worship God best, and what is there that prevents us from doing that?

It's a big question, and I am neither academically trained for such a task nor particularly gifted in this sort of writing. My writing has, for nearly 60 years, been that which paid the bills and supported the family. Even that, I believe, has been useful in writing this book. There's something about writing a speech for the president of a Fortune 100 company and taking input from a content committee of 27 engineers that makes almost any writing challenge less daunting.

Besides, attempting to delve more deeply into what, how, and why I believe is—to me—a useful way to spend a part of my latter years. From that, Essential Worship came.

Essential Worship is divided into four parts.

They are:

- Worship and its varieties.
- Four barriers to our best worship, each of which came from a question on my original list.
- Some thoughts on how we remove the barriers so that we may come to God with our best worship.

How We Got Here—and Why

Not many years ago, we developed a new ritual during our Sunday morning worship service. In an effort to attract and keep younger worshippers, we had inserted about seven minutes of praise choruses near the beginning of the service. The guitarists and the drummers would come up, and the praise team would lead the congregation in joyful song. Sometimes, in their enthusiasm, members of the praise team bounced up and down.

And that seemed to be a signal for one of our members—an older, gray-haired deacon—to bounce up and walk out. Guitars, drums, and music that wasn't yet a hundred years old weren't his idea of worship.

Since I was sitting in the choir, I got to watch this little pageant, and—since I knew that the member escaping the praise choruses was a committed Christian—I wondered what he was thinking.

He was thinking, as I learned later, that what we were doing was not worshiping, despite it being directed to God and in praise of God and despite any number of Biblical precedents for it. He had a firm definition of what worship was, and our seven or eight minutes of praise choruses didn't fit it.

This scenario was an extreme example of a common problem. We generally accept the culture into which we're born, its food, its language, and its definition of worship. In the culture into which I was born and have lived most of my life, the definition of worship varied but little from church to church, and almost not at all within a denomination. We went to church, and we did essentially the same thing every Sunday.

When we didn't, people like my friend got upset. What was happening did not fit their definition of worship.

As I pondered the questions in this book, I thought about this person, the veteran of nearly eighty years of church-going, a deacon, and a follower of Christ. I couldn't help but wonder if his mummified definition of worship, shared by more than a few, doesn't actually hinder what we're trying to do. And as I pondered more, I found that the definition—any definition—of worship is much more than the instruments that accompany us, the tempos of our songs, and even the words. In fact, what we do on Sunday may be just a small bit of the worship we should be offering God.

That is what Essential Worship is about: bringing our best worship to God. (In Chapter III, you'll find my attempt at a definition of worship.)

But next, because this book is much more personal than scholarly, I want to offer some background on my own worship journey.

I have had a long and varied relationship with worship. I have joined and/or attended worship services in the Presbyterian, Baptist (Missionary and Southern), Methodist, Pentecostal, and Episcopalian denominations. I also attended one and a half Unitarian services.

Each of the services was different, ranging from the participatory (the Episcopalian and the Pentecostal) to the passive (Presbyterian, Methodist, and Baptist). Some were more emotional, especially the Pentecostal, and most were more sedate. In the 1980s, we created even more divisions with the inclusion of Contemporary and Blended Worship.

However, they were all worship, and each one was appropriate and helpful at that time in my life; experiencing the different groups added something that carried me a step further. Certainly, each one of them broadened my definition of worship. Together they also provided a starting point for what brought me to Essential Worship.

I have also had a long relationship with the Bible. When I was three, my father was drafted into the Navy, and my young mother was left with nothing but me and a three-room apartment to care for. This had a number of outcomes, some better than others. For instance, Mother was a fan of Emily Post, and from a young age, I was taught manners that had never really made it into the social circles around Benson, North Carolina. On the other hand, I learned to read before I ever saw the inside of a classroom.

One of the books I had was a big, brown Bible storybook. Many of the stories came from the Old Testament and would now be considered too violent for very young minds. There was one, however, that had a picture showing Jesus sitting on a wall with his hand extended and about a half-dozen children gathered around him. The caption said: Suffer the little children to come unto me. Since my youthful lexicon had not yet admitted the concept of "allow" to my definition of "suffer," it was a while before I could understand the picture and caption. (I also believe that's one of the problems that we have when we deal with the Bible: we read a lot of things we don't understand.)

When I was about fifteen, already bookish and having a significantly over-inflated sense of my abilities, I began something that fell between a paraphrase and an explication of Matthew. A few years ago, I discovered it in a trunk, and looking at it with much more mature eyes confirmed that it was done by one far too young who knew far too little to even try such a thing.

I've also spent more than 40 years teaching Sunday School. Over the years, my classes included college students, adults, and finally, the class I taught for about ten years, the oldest group in our church. (The quip was that you went to Holmes' class and then to Heaven. It would have been funnier had it not been so true.)

During those years, I wrote several Sunday School courses, including one entitled, The Bible in Context, a survey of the entire Bible in 52 weeks. One of the high points in my Sunday School teaching career was when one of my class members, a man of almost 80 years, stopped me after class one day and thanked me for the course. It was, he said, the first time he had ever read through the Bible, and now he felt that he understood it better. I've carried that comment with me for years.

I studied each week so that I would have something to bring to the class on Sunday, and despite repeated culling, my bookshelves have an entire section filled with Bibles and large books explaining the Bible or teaching lessons from the Bible. I've found a lot of these helpful. I also discovered that some of the answers at which I had already arrived were wrong. For instance, I learned that my simple—and admittedly simplistic—explanation of the Trinity had been declared heresy in the Fourth Century.

I learned a lot of things from those classes, such as that there seems to be an infinite number of ways to pronounce "Laodicea." I also learned from my class members what it meant to have a deep faith when faced with an almost unimaginable pain or grief and to lean on God when there are no other resources.

All of these things informed the way I view worship. It is an act, as in taking communion or falling to one's knees in prayer. It's an attitude, as when we are filled by singing or hearing a hymn. It is a recognition of both the greatness of God above us and the closeness of God to us. However, I believe it goes further than that, attempting to recover at least some part of our oneness with God that we lost at the gates of Eden.

I believe that through our best worship, when our worship is neither an act nor an attitude but is at our very essence, we can come very close to doing that.

Worship, the Bible, and Me

Through the years, my family has had a lot of pets: three dogs, five cats, a bunch of fish, and a bird, to be specific. We have, except for the bird and most of the fish (who didn't live long enough for us to bond with), loved them all. We fed them, took them to the vet as needed, and tried to make their lives as comfortable as possible. In return, they—each in their own way—loved us back. True to their species, the dogs were much more appreciative of the affection they received, and the cats accepted it as their due.

The most heart-wrenching times were when we had to decide that the pet's health required a decision to end its life. With one, we waited far too long, extending BC's pain to avoid our own. We learned something from that. It was a mistake we didn't make again, although we wondered if we were making another mistake in the other direction.

Then we decided we would no longer have pets. As I told Linda, I was no longer emotionally able to make God-like decisions. She agreed.

That makes me wonder how God feels, that maybe He sometimes wonders if—given the reaction of His creation to Him—it might be just as well to have another creation.

I'm aware that this is not a perfect analogy. I did not, after all, create the dogs, cats, birds, or fish. We did, however, do the best we could with them, right up to the last decision. We were patient when they misbehaved. We were caring when they were in pain. I think this is an imitation, however pale, of how God deals with us.

I believe that we are loved by God, and—like the cats and dogs and maybe even the fish and the bird—we try to love Him back according to our species. We Christians do come in varied stripes, and those stripes often dictate how we respond to God.

I came to some sort of religious maturity around the middle of the twentieth century in a place where people were all pretty much alike. Most of the families had been in that area for more than a hundred years, and nobody in Benson had a last name that ended in a vowel until the Abdallas immigrated from Lebanon and the Delanos immigrated from Maine. We were, for the most part, church-going, Christ-believing Protestants. Since people usually adopt the culture into which they are born, the culture around my hometown was both supportive and comfortable.

Here Christians dealt in sureness and certainty, with hardly a sliver of doubt in any part of their faith. They had learned it at their mothers' knees and carried it unswervingly to their grave. They were unmoved and unbothered by those who were equally sure of other verities. They might, for instance, discuss the relative merits of baptism by sprinkling and baptism by immersion, but they probably would not move from their position at all.[1]

Within this broad group, there were significant variations, most of which could be found in my large extended family.

One who was not a member of my family was a deacon in our church. After I had learned enough Bible to make connections, he reminded me of the man praying in public in Matthew 6:5. He stood, he prayed, and he had a lot to talk to God about. Often he prayed so long that I'm sure that the preacher wondered whether there would be time for a sermon. In talking about the man who prayed in public with "many words," Jesus called him a hypocrite. For this man, I thought that was too harsh. Standing and praying lengthy prayers wasn't all that he did. He was also active in the work of the church. I didn't think he was a

---

[1] *This is a question that never really concerned me. By the time I was 16, I had been sprinkled (Presbyterian), immersed (Missionary Baptist), and baptized in the Holy Spirit (Pentecostal).*

hypocrite; however, I thought he probably subscribed to the theory that he would be heard for his many words.

Then there were Christians like my parents, who believed, were baptized, and did their best to live Christian lives. They both, at some point in their lives, taught Sunday School. Their concept of "Christian life," especially my father's, wasn't complicated. He worried about "right living" and didn't give much thought to the fuzzier parts of theology. Life to my father was much like a baseball game. You followed the rules. You played as well as you could. You were gracious in victory and stoic in defeat. With only a few exceptions, he could fit the teachings of Jesus into that frame. He also had a problem with people who adopted a pious attitude.

Mother's view was only a little more complex, especially later in her life. Christianity and its practice became much more about doing. If Mother saw a need, such as one of the students who rode on her school bus in need of clothes, she saw it as her duty to deal with it. There were merchants in Benson who probably hated to see her walk into the store, but she brought some sort of comfort to a lot of people. She was also named Humanitarian of the Year by one of the civic clubs. I thought of her as the embodiment of James 2:26: Faith without works is dead.

Our grandmother would have, in a much earlier time, been a good Pharisee. She was a rule-maker and a rule-keeper, and to her, religion was mostly about following the rules. Just as the Orthodox Jews had their 39 Sabbath Laws, Grandmother had an entire list that could be reduced to a single Sunday rule: don't have fun. Dancing, card games, movies, and any number of other activities that were acceptable Monday through Saturday were not—at least around Grandmother—acceptable on Sunday.[2] She didn't bother to explain the theological basis for these rules, and since Grandmother was Grandmother, we didn't ask.

There were, of course, others who approached their Christianity differently, such as the teenagers in our Baptist Training Union group, whose fervor waxed and waned but never really left them, young Christians who over time became much older Christians. Some of them are still in the same church and may well be occupying the same pews.

Or people like my uncle Ray, who approached everything in life with a sort of off-kilter smile and sometimes carried on a commentary on the sermon out of the side of his mouth. I don't think Ray's commitment was any less strong than any of the others; it was just different.

---

[2] *It was only much later that I realized that there was a real and important difference between grandmother's concept of Sunday rules and the Jewish Sabbath Laws. To follow the Sabbath Laws, the observer has to plan for the Sabbath. All of those things that were prohibited on the Sabbath had to be prepared for during the week. Grandmother's rules didn't really require any preparation; it was just don't do it.*

Each of these and their dozens of variations bring a different dimension to worship: the deacon's sometimes lecturing tone toward God, my parents' belief that their faith was somehow bound up in their works and actions, my uncle's commentary, and my grandmother's making up rules and seeing that everyone else kept them. They were, as they could, pointing their attention to God.

It became more complicated for me. I am one of those Christians who is a seeker but makes every effort to look like he's already found it. That's a dangerous attitude and one that requires frequent refreshments of humility. But there seem to be a lot of Christians who share my particular fault, Christians of all persuasions who make definite statements about indefinite ideas and stake out what they consider inviolable territories. This has been true through the centuries, but it has never been more visible than through social media, where a major concern seems to be whether Jesus was a Socialist.

There's really no profit in that. We don't fool anyone; almost everybody knows that we're not as smart or as sure as we're trying to sound. Too many scholars and sages over the years have approached the same sorts of questions with much greater humility. So I would like to assert here that I'm not certain of most of the ideas presented here. I'm sure in my faith in God and, through his Son, my salvation. I'm sure that God has given me more mercy than I deserve and more love than I can imagine. However, beyond the guaranties given in God's promises and communicated to me through the Bible, the ideas here are gleaned from my study and my experience. What I might consider the endpoint may be viewed by another as a beginning. Or by another as simply wrong.

What Is Worship

Worship is one of those words. When you say it, everyone knows what it means; it communicates. But when you try to define it, the definition is always too general, too specific, too large, or too small.

The internet, that repository of all information (if not knowledge and wisdom), offers this definition of worship:

> *Worship is commonly defined as follows (1): Noun- 1. The feeling or expression of reverence and adoration for a deity. 2. Adoration or devotion comparable to religious homage, shown toward a person or principle. Verb- 1. Show reverence and adoration for (a deity); honor with religious rites. 2. Treat (someone or something) with the reverence and adoration appropriate to a deity 3. Take part in a religious ceremony.*[3]

---

3 www.patheos.com/blogs/christiancrier/2014/08/26/bible-definition-of-worship-how-does-the-bible-define-worship/

It's a catch-all sort of definition, full of specifics and the obvious. And, if you look up adoration, it's defined as worship or veneration. In other words, worship is worship.

The "definition" describes worship rather than defining it, and then, I believe, it describes it incompletely, perhaps because our cries to God take so many different forms. Or no recognizable worship form at all.

My Bible Dictionary says that "worship is the honor, reverence, and homage paid to superior beings or powers, whether men, angels or God." It also says that worship is a translation of the Hebrew *shâlâh,* meaning to prostrate or bow down.[4]

This is helpful because it clearly positions the worshiper and the one worshipped, as when Joseph's brothers come before him in Egypt. They "bowed down to him with their faces on the ground."[5]

There are many obvious examples of worship in the Bible, and we'll look at some in the next few chapters. However, there are some that, to me, are not so obvious.

In 2 Samuel, just after the prophet Nathan has accused David of committing what David has declared a mortal sin, there are these verses:

---

[4] *The New International Dictionary of the Bible, (Grand Rapids: Zondervan Publishing,1987)1070*
[5] *Genesis 42:6b, (NIV)*

> *Yahweh struck the child that Uriah's wife had borne to David, and it fell gravely ill. David pleaded with Yahweh for the child; he kept a strict fast and went home and spent the night on the bare ground, covered with sacking.*[6]

David was pleading and bargaining with God for the life of his and Bathsheba's infant. He denied himself food and comfort. The royal officers watched him pour his agony out to God. The story continues:

> *On the seventh day the child died. David's officers were afraid to tell him the child was dead. "Even when the child was alive," they thought, "we reasoned with him and he would not listen to us. How can we tell him the child is dead? He will do something desperate." David, however, noticed that his officers were whispering among them themselves, and realized that the child was dead. "Is the child dead?" he asked the officers. They answered, "He is dead."*
>
> *David got up from the ground, bathed and anointed himself and put on fresh clothes. Then he went into the sanctuary of Yahweh and prostrated*

---

[6] *2 Samuel 12:15-16. (Jerusalem Bible)*

> *himself. On returning to his house, he asked for food to be set before him, and ate. His officers said, "Why are you acting like this? When the child was alive, you fasted and wept; now the child is dead you get up and take food." "When the child was alive," he answered, "I fasted and wept because I kept thinking, 'Who knows? Perhaps Yahweh will take pity on me and the child will live' But now he is dead, why should I fast? Can I bring him back again? I shall go to him, but he cannot come back to me."*[7]

The question might be asked: when is David actually worshipping, when he is denying himself and pleading with God or when he bathes, dresses, goes to the sanctuary, and then eats. They are very different actions, but in my opinion, they are both worship. In fact, they illustrate what I believe made David—an adulterer and a murderer—Israel's most revered king and a man after God's own heart.[8] When he prayed for the child's life, he recognized the sovereignty of God. When he accepted the child's death, he recognized the sovereignty of God. The circumstances changed, but neither God nor David's concept of God changed.

---

[7] *2 Samuel 12:18-23. (Jerusalem Bible)*
[8] *Acts 13:22*

(Years ago, I heard a preacher touch on something very similar that has stayed with me ever since. Our church orchestra was playing in a Spanish-language service, and as a courtesy, the preacher was preaching a sort of interlinear sermon. A paragraph in Spanish, then the same section in English. That was impressive, but what he said impressed me more: "If you pray for healing, and God heals, praise God!" He paused, said something in Spanish, then repeated it in English. "If you pray for healing, and God does not heal, praise God!" It was a concise summation of David's approach to God.)

So we have worship, formed or formless, vocal or without words, prescribed or spontaneous, collective or individual. We have worship in a virtually infinite variety, nearly defying definition.

Dr. Robert Webber in Ancient and Future Worship provides a memorable definition, calling to mind the most famous image in the Sistine Chapel ceiling: Adam reaching up to God, and God reaching down to Adam. Worship, says Webber, is in the space between the outstretched fingers of God and man. It is the connection.

As elegant as that definition is, it is still incomplete. That it exists is important. Why it exists is equally important. There is, I think, a purpose, something that compels us to worship.

Then, in the graphic definition, there is the question of who is reaching out to whom. Does man initiate worship? Does God cause man to initiate worship? Or does the worship of God come from God with man as its conduit?

So I will provide a definition of my own, one that I think will satisfy our needs here: Worship is our obeying God's call to us, continually bending toward and reaching out to Him. And we do that with a purpose.

In the beginning, there was no worship. It wasn't necessary. There was no distance between God and God's creations. Although Genesis doesn't say so, we can imagine that Adam and Eve walked with God in the cool of the day, sharing a perfect existence. In the beginning, God did not prescribe sacrifice and offerings, only obedience.

In a matter of a few sentences in Genesis, mankind went from being with God to being naked and ashamed, then being banished from their perfect existence and from their closeness to God. Since that time, we have worshipped, brought offerings, prayed, wept, and begged, all in our continuing attempt to once again achieve the closeness to God that we have lost.

But, the practical person who sometimes lives inside my head asks, "Can we do that?" The answer to that question is short and unsatisfying: I don't know. But I do believe that we can get much closer than we are now, that we can approach a worship that is at the very essence of our being, where our every decision and every act is worship.

Despite—or perhaps because of—the broad definition, we still need a framework for discussing the general subject of worship and its specific practice. Although this is none too precise, I believe it will serve. Worship may be divided into three categories, generally based on the impetus for the worship:

External: this is the worship that we recognize we are supposed to do, influenced by lessons learned at the very beginning of our religious observance. We give thanks to God for what we've received. We go to church; we say prayers; we participate in groups with others of our religion or denomination.

Internal: this is worship that springs from within us. This is David pleading and bargaining with God for the life of his son. Or Mary rejoicing after being told that she would bear the Son of God.

Essential: this is neither external nor internal in its source. It simply is. Neither does it have a past nor future tense; it exists only in the present. It exists only in the worshiper.

Each of these is—or can be—authentic worship, useful for connecting us to God. And, as we'll see in the next chapter, God honors the worship we're supposed to do as well the worship that we have to do. Or the worship that we are.

Worship from the Outside

In my bookcase is a 1945 copy of The Book of Common Prayer, a souvenir of my two-year experience as a High-Church Episcopalian. There's a bookmark at the Easter Day service, and I suppose that Easter was the last time I used it in church.

Here is one part of the service:

Christ is risen from the dead, and becomes the first fruits of them that slept.

For since by man came death, by man also came the resurrection of the dead.

For as in Adam all die, even so in Christ shall all be made alive.

Glory be to the Father, and to the Son, and to the Holy Ghost;

As it was in the beginning, is now, and ever shall be, world without end. Amen.

I don't remember this particular service, but I do remember the church in Asheville, with its soaring ceilings and tall windows. And I remember sitting and kneeling in the pews, reading the words, and being filled with awe in my surroundings and in the power of the service. The book that I was holding then and am holding now was ratified in 1790 and has been used in some form in Episcopal Churches ever since. The language is beautiful, and there are prayers for all sorts of circumstances and occasions, including a prayer of Thanksgiving after childbirth and a prayer for a sick person when there is small hope of recovery. It's designed as a kind of road map to reach out to God in whatever circumstances we might find ourselves.

Occasionally, I take it from the shelf, flip it open, and pray the first prayer I see, whether it's particularly appropriate or not. Each of the prayers is comforting and, to me, a sort of worship. It reminds me of what I am supposed to believe.

These prayers are, of course, all external; they don't arise from any particular need within us, except when we seek a prayer for a situation.

Praying these prayers is an act of worship. Or we may go to worship. Or we may simply worship, as we do when we go to worship. It is something we do, but we may not internalize it in any way, at least not at that time. The words of our mouth don't necessarily connect with the meditations of our heart. We might recite the Lord's Prayer while we mentally check the grocery list. And because we do it so easily and sometimes without further thought, it's easy to count such worship as trivial.

I don't think it is. Doing what we are supposed to is an important part of our continuing reaching for God. And the fact we use someone else's words or repeat our own day after day doesn't make it less worthy. I have said the same grace before meals for more than 25 years, sometimes varying it slightly for special occasions. There are prayers that worshiping Jews have been saying for thousands of years, just as God commanded them in the Old Testament to say them. I don't believe these are vain repetitions (something the Bible warns us about in Matthew 6:7.) As we'll see in just a moment, they may or may not be. It depends. The key seems to be not so much the words but what's behind the words.

The first worship in the Bible is recorded in Genesis 4, and in 16 very straightforward verses, we are told about the first offspring, the first offering, the first murder, and—in my opinion—the first great truth about worship.

Adam and Eve have been banished from Eden, and Eve has given birth to two sons: Cain and Abel. The language is spare, leaving much room for speculation[9], but the story is simple. In only 16 verses, we have a complete 3-act play.

This is the first act:

> *And in process of time it came to pass, that Cain brought of the fruit of the ground an offering unto the Lord. And Abel, he also brought of the firstlings of his flock and of the fat thereof. And the Lord had respect unto Abel and to his offering: But unto Cain and to his offering he had not respect. And Cain was very wroth, and his countenance fell.* [10]

In the second act, God speaks to Cain, asking why he is angry and downcast. "If you are well disposed, ought you not to lift up your head? but if you are ill-disposed, is not sin at the door like a crouching beast hungering for you which you must master?"[11] Strangely, Cain doesn't respond to God. He says to Abel, let us go out. And in the open field, he kills him.

In the third and final act, God speaks to Cain again. In a clear echo of God's conversation with

---

[9] *The Midrash is rich in explanations for various parts of this story, including an account of the marriage of the brothers and the subsequent killing of Abel. According to this opinion, each of the brothers was born with a twin sister, whom each brother married. Abel had a second sister who was desired by Cain. Abel would not agree to Cain's marrying her, and Cain murdered Abel.*

[10] *Genesis 4:3-4, (KJV)*

[11] *Genesis 4:6-7, (The Jerusalem Bible)*

Adam and Eve, God speaks, his creation dissembles, and God banishes his creation.

When the Cain-Able story came up in Sunday School lessons, the usual question was why did God accept Abel's offering but not Cain's. However, I think there is one that is substantially more basic and informs all of the other questions raised in the passage. It is: Why does God, who is omniscient, ask Adam and Eve and Cain questions to which God already knows the answers? God knows where Adam and Eve are and why they're hiding. He knows why Cain is upset. And he certainly knows, as he tells Cain, what has happened between the brothers. I believe that the question behind the question is how will Adam and Eve or Cain respond to God.

The truth of their (and in a broader sense, our) answers indicates our relationship with God. Neither Adam and Eve nor Cain faced God and their own shortcomings. They lied, made excuses, and proved themselves unworthy of closeness with God. They were banished, not because of their sin but because of their lack of repentance for that sin. It seems that the answers to all questions, including questions of worship and sacrifice, begin with us. Worship is a result of our devotion. It is symbolic of what we are really bringing to God.

Justin, the 2nd-Century churchman and martyr, in his defense of Christians, says in his First Apologia, "But we have received by tradition that God does not need the material offerings which men can give, seeing, indeed, that He Himself is the provider of all things." [12] That is, when you think about it, a very obvious statement. Since God created everything, he doesn't need man to bring him stuff.

Or, as C. S. Lewis puts it in Mere Christianity, "It is like a small child going to his father and saying, 'Daddy, give me sixpence to buy you a birthday present."[13]

It's obvious that it's not about what we bring to God, but how we bring it. As Justyn Martyr says, God "takes pleasure in those who imitate His properties."

These "properties" are made more specific in Deuteronomy 10:12. The passage reads:

> *And now, Israel, what doth*
> *the Lord thy God require of thee, but to*
> *fear the Lord thy God, to walk in all*
> *his ways, and to love him, and to*
> *serve the Lord thy God with all thy*
> *heart and with all thy soul. (KJV)*

Note that this is directed at Israel, the Lord's chosen people. It tells them what the Lord expects from them, corporately and individually. Missing

---

[12] *Justin Martyr, First Apologia, edited by Alexander Roberts, D.D. et al. (CreateSpace Independent Publishing, 2014) Chapter 10*

[13] *C.S. Lewis, Mere Christianity (New York, Harper-Collins, 2010) 143*

here, even though the details comprise much of the rest of the book, are sacrifice and worship. Very much present are verbs which connect us to God: fear God, walk in His ways, love Him, and serve Him.

This, then, is what I think is the first great rule of worship: It is not what we bring, but the depth of our devotion that causes us to act in imitation of His properties. In other words, devotion that causes us to act as God acts. Or, to quote Lewis again, as he writes in Mere Christianity, "we might think that God wanted simply obedience to a set of rules, whereas he really wants people of a particular sort."[14]

And this gives us some insight into the question that the people in my Sunday School class kept asking: Why did God accept Abel's offering but not Cain's? They both brought offerings, and so far as we can tell from the text, they both brought them voluntarily. The rules about offerings come hundreds of years later and are recorded in detail in Leviticus and Deuteronomy.

However, Cain brought "of the fruit of the ground." (The New International Version says, "some of the fruits of the soil.") It doesn't say whether they were particularly good or bad. On the other hand, Abel brought his firstlings or firstborn animals and some of the prescribed fat as his offering.

---

[14] *Mere Christianity, Page 78*

There are numerous mentions of "first fruits," "firstlings," and "firstborn" in the Old Testament. In Exodus 13:2, God commands that the people of Israel "consecrate to me every firstborn male. The first offspring of every womb among the Israelites belongs to me, whether human or animal."

This prevented the people of Israel from picking and choosing to find a sacrifice that they didn't mind giving to the Lord. It also recognizes that often the firstborn is dearest to us, as when God sent Abraham out to sacrifice Isaac. Abraham and Sarah had waited many years for Isaac, and the firstborn son was proof of God's covenant with Abraham, that he would become the father of many nations. The power of the story is that God is requiring the sacrifice of that which Abraham loves most.

But that's not all that the Lord requires. In Deuteronomy, it says, "You shall not sacrifice to the Lord your God an ox or a sheep which has a blemish or any defect, for that is a detestable thing to the Lord your God."

In other words, for our worship to be honored, we have to bring to God our very best.

Among the many church committees I have served on over the years, the only one I vowed never to serve on again was the Finance Committee. It is, of course, the one charged with setting the budget, taking the tithes and offerings, and determining how, within the missions of the church, to spend them. Inevitably, the tithes and offerings didn't reach the budget goals, and the church activities had to be modified accordingly. It was both a thankless and frustrating task, especially during our pledge drives.

Several of us had a moment of enlightenment when one of the committee members showed us some basic arithmetic he had done. He had taken the number of families in the church, assumed that each was a single-earner household, and multiplied it by the annual minimum wage. With those qualifications, if each family had tithed, we could have exceeded our budget goals. It was obvious that we were not "giving our best to the Master."

Tithing is a form of worship, but too often, we approach it as tipping God, giving him what is comfortable to us rather than what is required of us, the collection-plate version of "some of the fruits of the soil."

External worship is—at the same time—the easiest and the most difficult form of worship. Because it's prescriptive, we don't have to reach inside ourselves to find either a reason or method for worship. However, there is always the risk that it will become pro forma, simply something we do because it is something we do. Even as we read from the prayer book or say our usual grace before dinner, we are expected to bring to God our best.

Worship from the Inside

About forty years ago, I was driving through the mountains of North Carolina, tears streaming down my face, begging God to help me out. It seemed that nothing in my life was really going well. The most frequent line in my journals was "To be absent from the body is to be present with God."[15] In technical, psychological terms, I was a mess.

I had essentially given up and was asking God to figure it out. Fortunately, it was a long drive, and by the time I reached my destination, I was at peace. Nothing had really changed. Everything was still just as bad as it was when I started the trip. But I felt it was no longer just my responsibility, that I had help.

And I didn't even really know what I had prayed for. However, that didn't matter. As Paul wrote:

"Likewise the Spirit also helpeth our infirmities: for we know not what

[15] *This, like so many things in my memory, is a common misquote. The actual scripture is: Therefore we are always confident, knowing that, whilst we are at home in the body, we are absent from the Lord: 2 Corinthians 5:6 (KJV)*

> *we should pray for as we ought: but the Spirit itself maketh intercession for us with groanings which cannot be uttered."*[16]

I can't think of any greater proof of both the patience and love of God for his creation than his response to our internal worship, knowing that it happens when we are at the extremes of our emotions, either overwhelmed or overjoyed. From my experience, I believe we are more likely to reach out to God in our grief than in our gladness.

In his book, Extraordinary Stories, Dr. Don Pratt writes about what he calls the "Blues Psalms."[17] These psalms—about a quarter of the Psalter—are cries to God, born of exile and alienation. Things are not going the way the psalmist wants or expects them to. He's hurting, afraid, and needs help. Dr. Pratt notes that these are about three things: God, because God seems absent and doesn't seem concerned about what the psalmist is going through; himself (the psalmist), because he's hurting; and others, often his enemies.

But the psalmists are not the only ones prompted to cry out to God. Among others, there were the Old Testament prophets who were given tasks by God and didn't feel that they were getting sufficient support. They essentially accused God of poor management.

---

[16] *Romans 8:26 (King James Version)*

[17] *Don Pratt, Extraordinary Stories (Don Pratt, 2022) p. 54*

For instance, here is Habakkuk calling out to God:

> *O LORD, how long shall I cry, and thou wilt not hear! even cry out unto thee of violence, and thou wilt not save!*
>
> *Why dost thou shew me iniquity, and cause me to behold grievance? for spoiling and violence are before me: and there are that raise up strife and contention.*
>
> *Therefore the law is slacked, and judgment doth never go forth: for the wicked doth compass about the righteous; therefore wrong judgment proceedeth.*[18]

The Bible is full of examples, including Jeremiah, the prophet who complained so much that his name gave us the word "jeremiad," defined as a list of woes and complaints. However, internal worship is not just complaining, nor is it just singing the blues. The difference is in our expected outcome.

For instance, here's the beginning and the end of W.C. Handy's famous St. Louis Blues.

---

[18] *Habakkuk 1:2-4 (King James Version)*

I hate to see that evening sun go down,
I hate to see that evening sun go down,
'Cause my lovin' baby done left this town.

....

I got those St. Louis blues, I got the blues, I got the blues, I got the blues,
My man's got a heart like a rock cast in the sea, Or else he wouldn't have gone so far from me, lord, lord![19]

Notice that the narrator has the same problem at the end of the song that she had at the beginning. Nothing has changed except that the narrator may feel a bit better because she has vented. In contrast, here's god's response to Habakkuk's complaint: *I will work a work in your days, which ye will not believe, though it be told you.*

In other words, God told Habakkuk that He would answer Habakkuk's complaint in ways that the prophet wouldn't believe

It's the same with the blues psalms. The psalmist doesn't expect things to stay the same, no matter how bad they seem now. The psalmist in exile, sitting by the rivers of Babylon, looks

[19] *St. Louis Blues (W.C. Handy 1914) Public Domain*

beyond his pain to the time when the Lord treats Babylon as Babylon has treated the Jew.

For thousands of years, man has been calling out to God in his pain, expecting that God would come to his aid. It is sometimes the cry that comes from the depths of the individual's pain that most closely connects that person to God. We cry out to claim the His love and power to deal with our helplessness.

Recently, in an episode of a Hallmark Channel series, a character who had yearned for a child for years discovered that she was pregnant. She felt the child move in her womb. She woke her husband up and told him. He leapt out of bed, ran out the front door, and down the street, barefoot and in his pajama, shouting that they were going to have a baby.

Hallmark played the scene for laughs, but all I could think of was how Biblical it was. Hannah does much the same thing after she presents Samuel to Eli. Mary erupts in exultation after being visited by the angel. And Zachariah, the father of John, the Baptist, rejoices in song after he regains his voice. Everybody is happy that they're going to have a baby.

Bringing forth a son is only one reason for joyful worship in the Bible. There are other examples. But maybe we don't pay enough attention to them.

It seems strange that we seem more likely to cry out to God when we are overwhelmed than when we're overjoyed. After all, we should be happier to share good news and rejoice.

For some time, I wondered why that was true—or even if it was true. Then I realized that my concept of the greatness of God was inversely proportional to my estimate of how great I was. In good times, I felt large, powerful, and capable. God was there. I worshiped. But, I suppose I treated Him like the jack in the trunk of my car, to be used when necessary but not likely to be necessary.

It's not that I'm not grateful. I'm certain that I've been blessed far beyond anything I deserved. For instance, Linda and I have been married for more than sixty years. We've celebrated the good times and worked through the bad ones. Now we're coming toward the end of long lives, still hand-in-hand.

I often express my gratitude to Linda, most often for specific things she does to make my life easier. I sometimes congratulate myself for being a sufficiently acceptable husband that Linda stayed with me. And, in my prayers, I thank God for my marriage and my family.

It's this last part that I wonder about.

When we go out to dinner, and the server is skilled and attentive, I often—along with the tip—pay the server a compliment or express my gratitude for the service. Then we leave the restaurant, and I generally think no more about it. Unfortunately, my gratitude to God for his care for me for all these years may rise no higher than my compliments to the server. I fail to acknowledge that God created my wife and me, that God provided guidance all along our journey, and comfort when we felt alone and helpless. I fail to acknowledge that God has been central rather than peripheral to our marriage and to the family I'm so proud of.

It's not so much that I ignore God when things are right as I simply give him a nod.

That's not what the Bible teaches us.

I believe that one step on our path to essential worship is to give God credit for the good things in our life, to understand that our praise is as important as our plaint.

If our cry to God in our pain is a blues of a sort, then our cry when we are overjoyed should be an aria. It might be a deep and thoughtful recognition of the majesty of God, an exultant outpouring of praise, or a solemn acknowledgment of a long-awaited blessing delivered. There are dozens, perhaps hundreds of melodies for these arias, from the quiet to the grand, but they are all worship.

Consider, for instance, the psalmist—perhaps David—sitting on a hill on a dark, clear night, staring up at the stars that fill the sky in all directions. He feels very small in the vastness of God's creation, yet he recognizes that the same God who created the world cares for mankind, for him. The worship he feels on that starry night comes down to us as Psalm 8.

He sings out his praise to God, beginning with the highest points—the moon and the stars—and moving down to man, and then all other creation—all things under his feet. In the Psalm, there is awe, adoration, and appreciation, not in passing, but in grandeur. It begins and ends with "how excellent is thy name in all the earth!"

It might be profitable to stop for a moment and compare this with the most recent "words of your mouth" that praised God and expressed your gratefulness.

> *O Lord, our Lord, how excellent is thy name in all the earth! who hast set thy glory above the heavens.*
>
> *Out of the mouth of babes and suckling's hast thou ordained strength because of thine enemies, that thou mightest still the enemy and the avenger.*
>
> *When I consider thy heavens, the work of thy fingers, the moon and the stars, which thou hast ordained;*
>
> *What is man, that thou art mindful of him? and the son of man, that thou visitest him?*

For thou hast made him a little lower than the angels, and hast crowned him with glory and honour.

Thou madest him to have dominion over the works of thy hands; thou hast put all things under his feet:

All sheep and oxen, yea, and the beasts of the field;

The fowl of the air, and the fish of the sea, and whatsoever passeth through the paths of the seas.

O Lord our Lord, how excellent is thy name in all the earth![20]

When I read it, I can't help but contrast these words with my perfunctory "Thanks, God." It's not simply an acknowledgment and an appreciation. It is a longer, more poetic version of the child's blessing: "God is great. God is good." It is the greatness of God that assures us that his goodness is a part of our lives, and it is the goodness of God that assures us that his greatness will work for our good.

Or, as already noted, the worship that springs from inside us may be a cry of exultant joy, as when Mary responds to the angel's announcement that she will bear the Savior.

[20] *Psalm 8 (KJV)*

And Mary said:

> *My soul magnifies the Lord,*
> *And my spirit has rejoiced in God my Savior.*
> *For He has regarded the lowly state of His maidservant;*
> *For behold, henceforth all generations will call me blessed.*
> *For He who is mighty has done great things for me,*
> *And holy is His name.*
> *And His mercy is on those who fear Him*
> *From generation to generation.*[21]

Mary's worship—known as the Magnificat—is similar to the psalm in that it recognizes both the greatness and the goodness of God. It is different in that it is so personal. The psalmist recognizes God's creation and himself as a part of it, but Mary sees how it changes her life.

My favorite of these praises is a short outburst from Simeon when he recognizes the Christ child. Mary and Joseph have brought Jesus to the Temple on the eighth day after his birth, as commanded by the law. This is the account from Luke.

---

[21] *Luke 1:46-50 (NIV)*

And, behold, there was a man in Jerusalem, whose name was Simeon; and the same man was just and devout, waiting for the consolation of Israel: and the Holy Ghost was upon him.

And it was revealed unto him by the Holy Ghost, that he should not see death, before he had seen the Lord's Christ.

And he came by the Spirit into the temple: and when the parents brought in the child Jesus, to do for him after the custom of the law,

Then took he him up in his arms, and blessed God, and said,

Lord, now lettest thou thy servant depart in peace, according to thy word:

For mine eyes have seen thy salvation,

Which thou hast prepared before the face of all people;

A light to lighten the Gentiles, and the glory of thy people Israel.[22]

---

[22] *Luke 2:25-32 (KJV)*

This situation is similar to Hannah and Zachariah in that God brings about a long-awaited and long-hoped-for event. Hannah and Zachariah had given up; they were too old to have children. The thing I like about Simeon is that he never gave up. He had been told that he would see Christ before he died, and the Spirit guided him to the Temple that day.

Everything in the passage shows Simeon's devotion and obedience. Then it shows his reward: to hold the Christ child. And that's enough for Simeon. His life and his hopes have been fulfilled. "Lord, lettest thou thy servant depart in peace."

We don't know how long Simeon waited. He had been told that he would see the Christ, and that was evidently sufficient for him. He believed and continued to act on that belief, to regularly go to the Temple. Finally, in His own time, God delivered.

I would like to think I have a little bit of Simeon in me, the ability to recognize what God promises me, and the patience to wait for the fulfillment of that promise.

What I have termed "internal worship," the outpouring of our cry to God in our sorrow and in our joy is, I think, elemental; it's not a step before or beyond the externally-inspired worship we considered in the last chapter. It exists alongside external worship.

Neither is it complicated; it is not the result of Councils and assemblages. It is not prescribed. It is our individual response to terrible or wonderful times.

At its base, I think this worship takes us right back to the child's blessing: God is great; God is good. This is something we know, and it gives us the confidence to call on God rather than either struggle or rejoice alone.

Becoming Worship

Some years ago, I was trying to explain what was then my somewhat confused thoughts about essential worship to a friend over lunch. He listened patiently, and when I finished stumbling through the idea, he simply wiped his mouth on his napkin, looked me in the eye, and said, "I don't think you can do that."

I didn't have a particularly good answer for him then, nor do I now. Essential worship, where worship begins at the essence of our being, is the closing of the space between God and us, where we not only worship or do worship but are worship in our every act. It is not something you encounter frequently.

In fact, it may be aspirational, a reaching well beyond our grasp. However, if it is, I believe it's better to aspire and miss than to simply not try. After all, the reward of being even a little closer to God is great.

One thing that gave me hope was discovering the concept of total communion with God is not original with me. Some very smart people have already considered it.

I have already cited Lewis' Mere Christianity. Contrary to current usage, the word "mere" does not mean trifling or skimpy. It is better defined as "basic," or as the dictionary has it: apart from anything else; without additions or modifications. It has to do with what Lewis considers the essentials of Christianity, and one of these essentials is the wholeness of our worship. For instance, he goes beyond acts of worship to what might be termed essential worship.

> *I would rather say that every time you make a choice, you are turning the central part of you, the part that chooses into something a little different from what it was before.*[23]

The point is not what we do but what we are. When we decide to align ourselves with God, we change ourselves and diminish the space between us. Instead of worship leaping the space between the extended finger of God and the outstretched hand of man, it removes the space.

The way I envision God also makes me think that we can move much closer to him. I believe that when God banished Adam and Eve from the Garden, he didn't slam the door behind them. Instead, he waits for us to return, much like a

[23] *Mere Christianity, p. 91.*

parent who sits up listening for the child's car to turn into the driveway.

Since I was a child, I've heard sermons that concentrated on the angry God of the Old Testament, and there was a lot to preach from. Jack Nelson-Pallmeyer, in Jesus Against Christianity, quotes Walter Wink's accounting of Old Testament violence:

> *"...six hundred passages of explicit violence, one thousand verses where God's own violent actions are described, and a hundred passages where God irrationally kills or tries to kill for no apparent reason."*[24]

It's no wonder that so many believe that the God of the Old Testament (and possibly the New Testament) is disappointed in His creation and really prefers to keep His distance.

For centuries, scholars have attempted to justify, explain, harmonize, or simply disregard the violence depicted in the Bible. In doing so, they run into difficulties with Biblical authority, torture the text, or claim meanings that seem far from the received text.

Since I became an adult and spent time studying the Scriptures, I have taken a different approach. I recognize that there are vastly differ-

---

[24] *Jack Nelson-Pallmeyer, Jesus Against Christianity, (Harrisburg: Trinity Press International, 2001) 237*

ent views of God and His acts in the Bible. I also recognize that I can't explain how God can—at the same time—be an all-loving God and an angry God. Nor can I understand how the greatest act of love and the greatest act of violence were united at the cross.

I do know that the lens through which the writers of the Hebrew Bible viewed history was very different from ours; to them, history was God-caused. If the Jews prospered, it was because God was pleased with them. If they didn't, it was because their actions did not please God.

When Solomon finished building the Temple, God appeared to him and essentially gave him the rules of engagement:

> *"If my people, which are called by my name, shall humble themselves, and pray, and seek my face, and turn from their wicked ways; then will I hear from heaven, and will forgive their sin, and will heal their land."*[25]

When we encounter this passage, we usually read it as a promise: if we do what we're supposed to, God will hear us, save us, and heal us. It is, I suppose, a promise, but it cuts both ways, and in the view of the ancient Hebrews, when bad things

---

[25] *2 Chronicles 7:14 (KJV)*

happened, when the rains did not come, but the enemies did, they had offended a vengeful God.

At the risk of being accused of cherry-picking the Bible, I chose to put more emphasis on another promise, one that did not begin with an "if." It simply said that God loved his creation so much that he gave his son for us. If you look at how God relates to his creation in other passages, the loving God becomes more sharply defined than the angry God.

When he banishes Adam and Eve from the Garden, he removes them from their perfect life, but he sews clothes for them. They are not alone.

When Cain is banished for killing Abel, he pleads with God, saying that his life will be endangered; God gives him a mark to protect him.

When the Jews in the desert were thirsty, God provided water. When they were hungry, He provided food.

Throughout the Bible, there are examples of God taking care of his creation, sometimes in spite of their attitude. To me, the overreaching lesson is that God loves us, that He doesn't reject us even when we seem to reject Him, and He is never far away.

That gives me hope that there is such a thing as essential worship—or something very close to it.

The Bible provides several examples that might help us understand essential worship. One is Jesus in the Garden; another is Stephen.

When He goes to the garden, Jesus knows what is about to happen; He's already told his disciples. He knows that Judas will betray him, and Peter will deny him. He knows that the religious leaders are plotting against him. I think He also knows that while he is agonizing in prayer, His disciples, charged with keeping watch, have fallen asleep. Jesus is literally alone.

Matthew 26 tells us that:

> *And he went a little farther, and fell on his face, and prayed, saying, O my Father, if it be possible, let this cup pass from me: nevertheless not as I will, but as thou wilt.*[26]

Frightened. Alone. Too aware of the pain that he was facing, Jesus falls on his face and prays that—even though He wants another outcome—His Father's will be done.

There is no space between God and Jesus. There is no part of Jesus that inserts itself into this decision; Jesus submits to God and accepts God's will because he can do no other. Closeness to God is at his essence. Jesus' total submission

---

[26] *Matthew 26:39 (KJV)*

and His complete acceptance of God's will define essential worship.

However, there is a problem. Although this is the fully human Jesus praying in the garden, dreading what he knows is coming, it is also the fully divine Jesus. There is no space between him and God. In John 10:30, he tells us, "I and the Father are One."

Although, as Christians, we live in imitation of Christ, we know that it is a pale imitation, and for us to even approximate Jesus' submission to God is, I imagine, impossible. But I refer back to my previous point: the effort to close the space between our essential being and God, even if imperfect, will be beneficial.

The story of Stephen provides us with a more accessible example of essential worship.

We know something about Stephen, the first follower of Christ to be killed for his faith. He was—on the instructions of the Twelve—one of seven men chosen to make certain that the Greek widows were treated as well as the Hebrew widows in the distribution of food. The chosen seven were to be of honest report, full of the Holy Ghost and wisdom.[27] It was an administrative job, but it required administrators above reproach.

After being selected, the other six—Philip, Prochorus, Nicanor, Timon, Parmenas, and Nicolas—disappear from the account. However, the story of Stephen has just begun. Luke tells us

[27] *Acts 5:3 (KJV)*

that, full of the Spirit, he performs great signs and wonders, then gets taken before the religious establishment and is convicted on perjured testimony.

It's at this point that Stephen's story intersects with our point:

> *But he, being full of the Holy Ghost, looked up steadfastly into heaven, and saw the glory of God, and Jesus standing on the right hand of God,*
>
> *And said, Behold, I see the heavens opened, and the Son of man standing on the right hand of God.*
>
> *Then they cried out with a loud voice, and stopped their ears, and ran upon him with one accord,*
>
> *And cast him out of the city, and stoned him: and the witnesses laid down their clothes at a young man's feet, whose name was Saul.*
>
> *And they stoned Stephen, calling upon God, and saying, Lord Jesus, receive my spirit.*
>
> *And he kneeled down, and cried with a loud voice, Lord, lay not this sin*

> *to their charge. And when he had said this, he fell asleep.*[28]

Stephen, in this moment as in his life, proved himself to be full of the Spirit, ready to obey God, even unto a painful death.

There are three points in this passage that I find especially interesting. The first is that, according to the Scripture, Stephen was not felled with the stones. He, having seen Jesus and God in the Heavens, called on them to receive his spirit, then he knelt and said a one-sentence prayer.

The second is that Stephen sees Jesus standing at the right hand of God rather than seated. To me, he's waiting to receive Stephen and perhaps to be Stephen's advocate before God.

And finally, there is the reference to Saul. I have sometimes wondered what effect Stephen's dedication and courage might have had on the young man named Saul. Perhaps this was a necessary stop on the road to Damascus.

It's tempting to say that Stephen had achieved a level of essential worship. He followed Christ to the death. But the Scripture is clear that wasn't Stephen alone; he was full of the Spirit. He could say, "The Father, the Son, and I are one." Perhaps that's the most concise expression of essential worship.

---

[28] *Acts 7:55-60 (KJV)*

Baby Steps and Half Measures

If we agree that essential worship is a possibility or at least a worthy aspirational goal, the obvious question is what prevents us from achieving at least some part of our goal.

The first thing that comes to mind is a line I often used in dealing with clients who sometimes failed to appreciate the skills involved in writing copy. "If it were easy, everybody would want to do it."

It's not easy, and I believe that human beings, even though we are created in the image of God, are not able to completely give ourselves to God without strenuous effort. It's just not the human way.

There are, I think, at least three large obstacles to essential worship, and they all have the same origin. They can be summed up in two very similar words with opposite meanings: arrogate and abrogate.

Arrogate means to take or claim something without justification. Abrogate means to evade a responsibility or duty. I believe that, unfortunately, these two words succinctly describe what stands between us and essential worship. We arrogate prerogatives that belong to God alone, and we abrogate responsibilities that he has assigned us. I also believe that for the most part these problems fall in three specific areas.

However, before getting into three specifics, let's consider one obstacle that should be obvious but seldom is: Seeking essential worship is a matter of commitment.

The German Jewish writer and theologian Martin Buber wrote extensively about the I and Thou, a relationship set apart from the more common I and It. According to Buber, the I-It relationship objectifies the It. It is a thing with which we have a relation. To me, an example of this is when we go to worship. According to Buber, the I-It relationship cannot be experienced with the whole being.

On the other hand, the I-Thou relationship cannot be experienced any other way: it is only experienced when we commit our whole selves to it, giving and taking the relationship. In all of I-Thou, Buber emphasizes that the relationship is a mutual giving, not one active party worshipping and a passive party receiving. As we move from I-It to I-thou, we meld our realities with God's.

Worship, especially essential worship, is not a matter of half measures; it is a wholehearted commitment.

Perhaps it would be useful to take an inventory of our attitudes before going forward, to determine what will be required of us to make such a commitment.

The first question is, I believe, whether we are really seeking God's will. When we make a decision, what factors other than God's will are we considering?

My father, who—as I have already mentioned—had a small tolerance for piety, wondered to me one day why it seemed that God only called our preachers to larger and better-paying churches. I didn't have an answer for him. I still don't.

I can't help but believe that there are a host of factors even the most dedicated pastor considers when he considers a move. He is, after all, only human.

This means that the pastor has the same problems we have, perhaps with a difference of degree.

The second question, closely related to the first, is what are our priorities? What do we seek most from the decision?

For the first decade after I graduated from college, I changed jobs about every eighteen months, on average. Thinking back over those decisions, I wondered if God's will entered into them at all. In fact, I might have denied that God cared where I worked.

My priorities were to support my young family, to find work that wasn't terribly boring, and perhaps to inch closer to the goals I had when I graduated from college.

We spared a little time for God. We went to church and participated in its activities. Most of our social group came from church. We put something in the collection plate.

But I don't remember asking God what I should do, perhaps because I was afraid God would give me an answer I didn't want. I wasn't anywhere near Christ's agonized prayer in the Garden.

Step one, I think, is to make sure that when we pray "thy will be done," we mean it. When we are wholeheartedly dedicated to that, we can attack the other obstacles in our path.

Those obstacles are what most of the rest of this book is about. What they are, and what we can do to remove them. In each case, God has said, "Don't do that!" And in each case, we still do.

Job and Jonah

For years, I have thought there was some sort of commonality between the Old Testament books of Job and Jonah, but the more I studied, the more I recognized the differences between the two books.

After all, Jonah is a Hebrew prophet. Job isn't even a Hebrew.

The Book of Jonah is a short, straightforward story with a small cast. There's God, Jonah, the fish, a chorus of sailors, and the worm. Job, on the other hand, is a long story with a much larger cast: God, Satan, Job, his wife, his so-called friends, and the young man who comes in to tell the elders that they are wrong.

And then there's the condition of the title character at the end of the story. When we last see Jonah, he's saying, "And I'm so angry I wish I were dead."[29] Job, on the other hand, has had his riches restored to him, he has a family, and God has told his friends off. Job's outlook going forward is considerably brighter than Jonah's.

But these are, I think, just details. The big difference is in the questions they address. In Job,

---

[29] *Jonah 4:9b (NIV)*

the question is, "Why do bad things happen to good people." In Jonah, it's, "Why do good things happen to bad people." The Scriptures leave no doubt that Job is good and the Ninevites are very bad.

The Bible often presents its lessons in the most dramatic terms, just so that the slower among us don't miss the point. For instance, Jesus used the parable of the Good Samaritan rather than the good Jew. For most of his audience, a good Jew would not have been either a surprise or instructive. However, by making a Samaritan—a person from a race despised by the Jews—the hero of the story, Jesus made the point very clear.

The same thing is true in Job and Jonah. Job is a well-defined example of "good people." In the prolog, the Bible says, "There was a man in the land of Uz, whose name was Job; and that man was perfect and upright, and one that feared God, and eschewed evil."[30] A few verses down, God, speaking to Satan, repeats those exact words. So we're told twice in eight verses that Job is "perfect and upright." Then God fingers Job, and Job's problems begin.

In the book of Jonah, when God sends the prophet to Nineveh, He's sending him to a people known throughout their part of the world for their violence and cruelty. It was said that they would cut off both of a captive's legs and one arm, "leav-

---

[30] *Job 1:1 (KJV)*

ing the other arm and hand so that they could shake the victim's hand in mockery as he was dying."[31]

The message is clear. Job: good. Ninevites: bad. Yet God allows Satan to destroy Job's life, and he dispatches Jonah to save the hated Assyrians. Neither Job nor Jonah was pleased with God's actions.

And in that, I found the commonality that I was looking for. Both Job and Jonah had their own version of God. They had a vision of how their God should act, and God was not acting according to their scripts. They had gone from beings created in the image of God to beings creating their own image of God.

In other words, they wanted to tell God what to do. And God answered them.

In Jonah, as with the rest of the story, it's straightforward. God has rescued Jonah from the big fish, and Jonah has gone through Nineveh, preaching repentance. The scripture records the Ninevites' response:

> *For word came unto the king of Nineveh, and he arose from his throne, and he laid his robe from him, and covered him with sackcloth, and sat in ashes.*

[31] *Timothy Keller, Rediscovering Jonah, (Penguin Books, 2020) 11*

> *And he caused it to be proclaimed and published through Nineveh by the decree of the king and his nobles, saying, Let neither man nor beast, herd nor flock, taste anything: let them not feed, nor drink water:*
>
> *But let man and beast be covered with sackcloth, and cry mightily unto God: yea, let them turn everyone from his evil way, and from the violence that is in their hands.*
>
> *Who can tell if God will turn and repent, and turn away from his fierce anger, that we perish not?*[32]

Jonah, under duress, does what God has commanded him to do: to go through Nineveh and call for repentance.[33] The king decreed that the Ninevites engage in mourning and that they "turn everyone from his evil way." To me, it's important (even if it's often overlooked) that the king did this not as a transaction (Repent and I won't destroy you.) but in faith.

"Who can tell?" he asks. He does the right thing even though the outcome is uncertain.

---

[32] *Jonah 3: 6-9 (KJV)*

[33] *It's interesting to me that God was calling for them to repent, i.e. change their behaviors, rather than to convert. I think that there is a lesson in that for our witness.*

The story could have ended right there. In fact, it would have been better for Jonah's reputation through the centuries if it had. He had, after a dramatic false start, done as God had commanded. The Ninevites, famous for their cruelty, had repented, and Jonah had been successful. But Jonah, sullen prophet that he was, wouldn't simply accept success. Instead of taking a victory lap, he goes outside the city, and in what the Bible calls a prayer, he says:

> *I pray thee, O Lord, was not this my saying, when I was yet in my country? Therefore I fled before unto Tarshish: for I knew that thou art a gracious God, and merciful, slow to anger, and of great kindness, and repentest thee of the evil.*
>
> *Therefore now, O Lord, take, I beseech thee, my life from me; for it is better for me to die than to live.*[34]

There is almost too much irony here. Jonah, who has defied God and has been saved from death by God, is angry at God for being "merciful, slow to anger, and of great kindness." So far as he is concerned, the Ninevites, famous for their cruelty and their evil ways are getting an undeserved reprieve from the judgment of God.

---

[34] *Jonah 4:2-3 (KJV)*

That is not, according to Jonah, the way God is supposed to work. The problem is, in a phrase that became politically popular in some circles, he wasn't "hurting the people he was supposed to hurt." Jonah was a Jew, one of God's chosen people. The Ninevites were not. The right thing to do, according to Jonah, was to smite them.

Finding the parallel to Jonah's bitter prayer in Job is difficult. In fact, almost everything about the Book of Job is difficult. Several of the commentaries that I've read have a disclaimer somewhere near the front that says that the translation of some verses is unreliable and that some sentences didn't make it from the Hebrew to an early translation; the translator had evidently just given up.

Most of the pages of Job in my NIV Study Bible have a footnote that offers alternate readings of the Hebrew or simply says "the meaning of the Hebrew phrase is uncertain." According to Harold Kushner, "Job uses more words that occur nowhere else in the Bible than virtually any other book."[35]

Years ago, when I was cobbling together a dramatic version of the book of Job for my Sunday School students, I encountered another difficulty. Job's final speech is Chapters 27-31. Then God's answer to Job begins in Chapter 38. The

---

[35] *Harold S. Kushner, The Book of Job When Bad Things Happen to a Good Person, (New York: Trinity Press International, 2001)237*

chapters between 31 and 38 are speeches by a young man named Elihu, whom we haven't met before. I wondered then if Elihu was a later addition, perhaps by a scribe who didn't think God had been defended effectively.

Whatever the difficulties, it is clear that Job—after dealing with his friends for days—complains to God, much as Jonah did. However, true to the structure of the books, Job's complaint is much more complex. Where Jonah whines, then goes outside the city to pout, Job, despite his misery, stands his ground.

In my reading, Job goes through a range of emotions in his complaint: defiance, justification, and resignation. Although one follows the other, the difference in tone is obvious, and for all of its emotion, his speech is as carefully constructed as a lawyer's closing statement.

It starts just after Bildad's last speech. Bildad, one of the three "comforters," says, "How then can man be justified with God? or how can he be clean that is born of a woman?"[36] This has been the thread that has—with various levels of accusation and intensity—gone through all of the counsel of Job's friends. Their argument is very logical:

If God is just (and we know He is)

He does not afflict the righteous.

You are afflicted, therefore, you must not be righteous.

---

[36] *Job 25:4 (KJV)*

I think at this point, Job had had enough. He had lost his family, his wealth, and the respect of his neighbors; now, he has been told once again that he is the author of his own afflictions. You can feel the heat of his temper in his words:

> *How hast thou helped him that is without power? how savest thou the arm that hath no strength?*
>
> *How hast thou counselled him that hath no wisdom? and how hast thou plentifully declared the thing as it is?*
>
> *To whom hast thou uttered words? and whose spirit came from thee?*[37]

Then he makes a declaration that is not a complaint, but a challenge. Here I picture Job not only shaking his fist at the three friends who have spent days giving him advice but also at God. He says:

> *As God liveth, who hath taken away my judgment; and the Almighty, who hath vexed my soul;*
>
> *All the while my breath is in me, and the spirit of God is in my nostrils;*

---

[37] *Job 26:2-4*

> *My lips shall not speak wickedness, nor my tongue utter deceit.*
>
> *God forbid that I should justify you: till I die I will not remove mine integrity from me.*[38]

Here he defies anyone to change him from the man he believes himself to be. When I read this, I marvel at Job's courage. There he is, in the ashes, with everyone he knows—his friends, his neighbors, his wife—arrayed against him, and he swears the most serious oath he knows. "As God liveth," he says, acknowledging that God has taken away all that he has. But, still, he will be honest and upright.

In Chapter 29, Job moves from defiance to justification. I think his voice grows softer, and his gaze turns more inward. It sounds like he's not so much talking to the three men sitting with him as to himself.

This section is also in three parts. In the first part, he recalls how good his life used to be. He was rich. He was surrounded by family. He was respected. In short, he had everything a man could ask for.

---

[38] *Job 27:2-5 (KJV) Kushner and others contend that these verses are the words of Job, but the rest of this chapter and the following chapter—a poem on Wisdom—are not connected with Job's defense. The balance of Chapter 27 is considered by some to be the lost speech of Zophar.*

Then he moves to the second part, contrasting the good life with what his life has become. All that he had that was good has been replaced by bad. He catalogs the good deeds he has done.

And finally, he makes what one might call a "negative confession." He lists all of the sins that he has not committed. It's an impressive list, including lust, lying, not honoring his marriage, being unjust, ignoring the needy, especially widows and orphans, worshipping other gods, rejoicing in the misfortune of his enemies, and refusing hospitality to strangers. It's a list that should make most of us who read it seriously uncomfortable.

Job says, "These are things I didn't do."

And he asks for a fair trial, that his accuser detail exactly what his wrongdoing is. If his accuser hands down an indictment, he says "Surely I would take it upon my shoulder, and bind it as a crown to me."[39] Job does not fear whatever charges God might bring against him.

Having made this declaration, he adopts a tone of resignation. He says:

> *38 If my land cry against me, or that the furrows likewise thereof complain;*

[39] *Job 31:36 (KJV)*

> *39 If I have eaten the fruits thereof without money, or have caused the owners thereof to lose their life:*
>
> *40 Let thistles grow instead of wheat, and cockle instead of barley."*[40]

Job declares his innocence, but says that if he is guilty, he will accept his punishment.

Then the Scripture says, "The words of Job are ended." I read that as Job saying, "I rest my case. I have presented my evidence. I want a fair trial. And I will accept the verdict."

Much has been written about the "patience of Job" or his lack of patience. Here, I'm more interested in the courage of Job, a man essentially without allies and separated from his God, assaulted physically and psychologically. Yet, he stands, maintaining that none of this will make him abandon his integrity.

As with Jonah, the challenge is not without irony. Satan accuses Job of being righteous because God has been good to him. Job turns that on its head, declaring that God should be good to him because he has been righteous. The only thing that they differ on is which is the cause and which is the effect.

However, both of them see the relationship as transactional. There are tinges here of the pros-

[40] *Job 31:38-40 (KJV)*

perity gospel. And we finally get to the commonality between Jonah and Job. They worshipped God, but he was the God of their conception. Jonah's God honored the covenant that He had made with the Jews to the exclusion of the evil Ninevites. Job's God recognized righteousness and rewarded the righteous. That was the contract.

Then God answered them and gave both of them the same message: you don't understand.

My understanding that I didn't understand may have been responsible for one of the most profound statements I ever made to a Sunday School class. It was in the beginning days of the Prosperity Gospel, and I had been warning the class against the "vending machine" concept of God ("Insert prayer, receive favor").

The class consisted of about twenty bright, young college students, and although I taught the lesson for each Sunday, the person who wrote that lesson might not have recognized it. Every Sunday was an energetic discussion, and sometimes it ranged far afield. One of my favorite class members was a young man who was studying at Emory. He was very smart and was noted locally for having almost no filter on his mouth. When I said that we should not worship in anticipation of some sort of reward or payment, he raised his hand, and asked, "Then why do you worship Him?"

With a similar lack of filters and not a lot of thought, I said, "Because He's God, and I'm not!" Then it took thirty-plus years for me to see what that had to do with Jonah and Job. I believe that, as curt and possibly thoughtless as my answer was, I had concisely summed up God's answer to both Job and Jonah.

Jonah complained to God, he got angry at God's mercy, and he went and sulked. The sun was hot, so God made a plant that shaded him. The King James Version says that "Jonah was exceedingly glad of the gourd."[41] It was, however briefly, Jonah's version of Job's good life. Shaded and comfortable.

The next day, God made a worm that attacked the plant and caused it to die. On top of that, He sent a "vehement east wind" and the hot sun. Jonah was no longer comfortable; it was, again very briefly, the parallel to the time when Job had lost his good life.

Jonah and Job each decided that they had rather be dead than live that way. Jonah tells God that he's angry "even to the point of death." Job goes even further and curses the day that he was born.

And God answers them both. To Jonah, in a lesson appropriate to the short and simple story, he points out that Jonah was angry because the gourd died, but he didn't create it, nor did he labor over it. Then he asks how Jonah could

---

[41] *Jonah 4: 6b (KJV)*

mourn the plant he didn't create, but not the 120,000 Ninevites who were blundering dumbly through their lives and didn't know their right hand from their left hand. It is left unsaid, but is understood that these people, their cattle, and all of the world around them were God's creation.

God's answer to Job, again in keeping with the longer and more complex story, is a grand tour of his creation. God speaks forcefully to Job, asking him if he could create anything like that. And Job, both awed and embarrassed, admits that he couldn't, and says he will speak no more.

We don't know if Jonah took God's point or not; his response is not recorded, and we don't hear of him being dispatched to other cities to preach repentance. However, the Scriptures leave no doubt that Job learned his lesson. He retracted his demands, and God not only returned to him all of the things that had made his life good and comfortable but scolded those friends who, however good their intentions, had heaped blame on Job.

It turns out that my intuitive linkage between Job and Jonah did exist. In fact, it becomes pretty obvious. Both of them complain to God that He's not being fair to them. And God tells both of them that He's God, and they're not, that they should not confuse the Creator and the creation, that we do not worship God according to our definition.

Isaiah warns us against this sort of arrogance. "Woe to you who strive with your Maker, earthen vessels with the potter! Does the clay say to the one who fashions it, 'What are you making'? or 'Your work has no handles'?"[42] It is enough that God has created us; it is too much that we attempt to make definitions, rules, and boundaries.

Nor is it good for us to judge the godliness of God's actions. Recently, I was challenged by a young man who styled himself as an atheist. After cataloging a rather lengthy list of everything that was wrong in the world, from deformed babies to families dying from hunger, he asked, "How can you worship an omnipotent God who allows these things to happen?"

I told him I didn't know why there was evil in this world. I didn't even know why there was good. I did know that I believed in a God that knew much more than I did. Again, on reflection, I think I may have approached profundity. Simply by saying, "I don't know."

The young man was, in my opinion, making nearly the same mistake Jonah and Job made. But it wasn't exactly the same. Neither Job nor Jonah denied the existence of God, even as they tried to set their own boundaries. They did, like the young man, want a God who behaved according to their rules.

---

[42] *Isaiah 45:9 (New Revised Standard Version)*

There is another example that I think is more in keeping with our search for essential worship. Many years ago I had a friend, a seminary graduate who after serving as a pastor became a hospital chaplain. He spent his days comforting people who had or were about to suffer loss. He was well-suited to the position, a person of great empathy and a calm demeanor.

Then his wife became pregnant with their first child. The child was born, and we celebrated with them. However, in a few days, the child died, and the doctors couldn't explain why. Some years later, he told me how angry he had gotten with God, how he had silently screamed at God for giving them such great joy and allowing it to be yanked away from them so terribly.

Yet, he never stopped believing. He never left his calling. However, it took years for him to assuage his anger. He was, like Jonah, angry unto death and like Job, swearing that "as the Lord lives," he would not give up his integrity. I think my friend was in a centuries-old line of people who might shake their fists at the heavens, but who will still believe and seek closeness with God.

Job and Jonah are examples of what I think is the overarching impediment to our approaching essential worship: we are tempted to define the God in whom we believe. Essential worship does not allow for an employment application that God must submit before we worship. It is we who must submit. As it says in Isaiah: But now, O LORD, thou art our father; we are the clay, and thou our potter; and we all are the work of thy hand.[43]

[43] *Isaiah 64:8 (KJV)*

Claiming What Isn't Ours

I've already noted that my father wasn't a fan of public displays of piety. Nor was he given to outbursts, especially of anger. But when I was in my early twenties, I witnessed a scene that gave me a new insight into his personality. And maybe his belief system.

The fact that his actions were so unusual made it memorable, but it wasn't until I was thinking about this chapter that I realized what had really happened.

In the small town where I grew up, we didn't have many scandals, and most of those we did have were hidden from public view. Occasionally someone would stray from the marital bounds, and in at least one instance, a store owner went into bankruptcy. But mostly we followed the rules.

That's part of the reason it caused such a stir when a local preacher went to another state with a woman not his wife.

I don't remember the details of the situation, but I do know that the preacher was a man whom Dad respected. The preacher worked with Dad in the store during the week and on Sundays, he preached at a charismatic church. He occasionally scolded Dad for playing baseball on Sunday afternoons. Overall, this man embodied what Dad thought a Christian should be: humble, quick to help anybody who needed help, and more strict with his own actions than he expected others to be with theirs.

Until, suddenly, he was gone.

Then the judges came out in force. Some contented themselves with quiet tut-tutting, but many others became very vocal. They had, they said, seen this sort of flaw in the preacher's character a long time ago. Or, he had been hiding a perverse nature behind all that preaching.

Among those who didn't participate in the blanket condemnation of the preacher were the editor of the local paper and my own father. I didn't expect him to stand up for the preacher; I expected him to simply say nothing. That was his way.

However, I and a couple of other people discovered we were wrong. Someone was roundly condemning the preacher not so much for leaving town with another woman but for disappointing a lot of people, and for the only time I can remember, my father lost it. He didn't raise his voice, but he put a sharp edge on it that told anybody listening that he was angry. He reminded the speaker that the preacher had for years lived his beliefs, that he was a man that Dad had respected and still did, and if he committed this uncharacteristic act, Dad would neither judge nor criticize him for it. And unless the speaker had lived a blameless life, he should do the same thing.

Dad may have, in that three or four minutes, uttered more words in anger than he had in the rest of his life. I remember that I was proud of him for standing up to people he knew he was going to have to see every day. And while Dad got over his anger, I doubt he ever thought the same about the people he aimed it at.

Without realizing it, Dad was reenacting a scene from the New Testament, where Jesus told the crowd who wanted to stone the sinful woman that he who is without sin should cast the first stone. As in the biblical scene, the stone-throwers turned and walked away. The fact that Dad looked like a coiled spring may have had something to do with it.

Also without realizing it, Dad was battling what I think is a major obstacle to our essential worship: self-righteousness, also known as sanctimonious, holier-than-thou, smug, complacent, pietistic, Pharisaic, and unctuous. It denotes someone who believes that they hold the moral high ground, no matter how thin the evidence.

And certainly, it was a battle worth fighting. One pastor has called self-righteousness "the worst disease ever to afflict the human race."[44] I

[44]*escapetoreality.org/2021/08/05/signs-of-a-self-righteous-mind set*

wonder if that's not an overstatement, but certainly, it ranks among the worst, not only because of what it does to the self-righteous person but also because of what it does to our witness.

Self-righteousness repels people, making it difficult, if not impossible to get them to be open to what Christ can do in their lives

In terms of our worship, a self-righteous attitude creates at least three problems: it mistakenly arrogates (as Job and Jonah did) a quality that belongs to God and not to us, it makes us resistant to instruction, and it focuses us in the wrong direction.

According to the Scriptures, there's really no such thing as "self-righteousness," there is only the delusion of it. As Paul writes, in his Letter to the Romans, "There is none righteous, no not one."[45]

And because we think we are righteous, we are stubborn and proud, resistant to instruction. In our proud and stiff-necked manner, we do not follow God's direction.[46]

And, finally, it focuses us in the wrong direction. First, our focus contrasts us with those around us. Our concentration is on people, not on God. It also focuses us on the act rather than the

---

[45] *Romans 3:10 (KJV)*

[46] *In the Scripture, "stiff-necked" is often used as a synonym for "proud." The image comes from an ox that could not have its head turned by the driver who was attempting to guide it by poking its neck with a goad. Stiff-necked means that the beast doesn't go where it is directed, just as we, in our pride, don't go where God leads us.*

attitude. We go about doing "good" and seeking approval. We are using those around us to reflect our self-approval of ourselves back to ourselves. Self-righteousness prevents us from understanding that it is not the act, but our attitude in performing the act, and it's not between the actor and man, but the actor and God.

The perfect portrait of the self-righteous man is in Jesus' parable of the two men who went to pray. Jesus prefaces this parable with this:

> *"To some who were confident of their own righteousness and looked down on everyone else, Jesus told this parable."*

One man, the Pharisee, "stood and prayed thus with himself, God, I thank thee, that I am not as other men are, extortioners, unjust, adulterers, or even as this publican. I fast twice in the week, I give tithes of all that I possess."[47]

Notice that he is proud of his righteousness, keeping the law, and scorning those around him.

Jesus contrasts the prayer of the Pharisee with the prayer of the publican, who "would not lift up so much as his eyes unto heaven, but smote upon his breast, saying, God be merciful to me a sinner."

---

[47] *Luke 18:11 (KJV)*

It is not unusual for Jesus to sharpen the point of his parables by creating the cast from the edges of society. In the parable of the Good Samaritan, the man who is robbed is saved by the Samaritan, not by the religious people who walked by him and averted their eyes. In the parable of Dives and Lazarus, it is the very rich man and the beggar. Here we have the same sort of comparison: the most religious person and the most despised, a civic leader and a tax collector.

The Scriptures present several instances of Jesus criticizing the Pharisees for obeying the law while essentially ignoring God. They tithe spices without rendering "justice, mercy, and faithfulness." They loved the best seats in the synagogue. They observed the sabbath, keeping strictly to the Sabbath laws while ignoring those who were suffering on the Sabbath.

They were proud that they were not as other men.

For those with any familiarity with the New Testament, any discussion about self-righteousness immediately goes to the Pharisees. In fact, as noted above, "pharisaic" has become an accepted synonym for "self-righteous." However, if we're not careful, we read about the Pharisee, and smugly thank God that we're not like him.

Those with a greater familiarity with the New Testament are more cautious, realizing that it's possible—and I believe it's probable—that the Pharisees got a bad rap in the New Testament. On the one hand, there is the question of whether the writers of the Gospels, writing years after the crucifixion, provide an unbiased account.[48] The Christians were, after all, in competition with the Jews. Additionally, the attitudes of the writers often color—sometimes obviously—how they present the religious establishment. (For instance, Matthew's gospel calls out the Pharisees for opposing Jesus (Matthew 12:22-36) while Mark says that the opposers were scribes (Mark 3:22). In Matthew, John, the Baptist calls the "Pharisees and Sadducees" a brood of vipers (Matthew 3:7), But in Luke, it is "the crowd" who is a brood of vipers.)

We do know that the Pharisees were, after all, very religious people, following both the oral and written law. I also believe that a group of Pharisees would probably be very much like the usual church congregation, with some members being loving and helping and others being stiff-necked and judgmental. It's sometimes overlooked that there are "good" Pharisees mentioned in the New Testament. In fact, some Pharisees became powerful in the early Christian church and were influential in defining Christianity.[49]

---

[48] *Frederick Murphy provides an excellent summary in the scriptural problems with the presentation of the Pharisees in his book Early Judaism: The Exile to the Time of Jesus, pp. 213-244. Much of what's presented here comes from Murphy's book.*

[49] *See Acts 15:5 for a reference to a debate between Paul and his allies and a group of Christian Pharisees regarding the circumcision of converts.*

Nicodemus and Joseph of Arimathea, for instance, were both high-ranking Pharisees and members of the Sanhedrin, the ruling body of the Jews. Nicodemus is introduced in the third chapter of John, and it is in his conversation with Jesus that Jesus explains the concept of being born again. It is also in this conversation that Jesus pronounces what may be the most famous verse in the New Testament: John 3:16. Nicodemus and Joseph of Arimathea provided the place for Jesus' burial and the combination of spices and perfumes used to prepare the body for burial.

In Acts 15, Gamaliel, who was Paul's teacher, is credited with saving the lives of Peter and the other apostles by cautioning the Sanhedrin against putting them to death. While his counsel was not a declaration of faith, it was effective in saving the apostles' lives.

But certainly, the most influential Pharisee in the New Testament is Paul, and he was, at best, an unlikely convert. As noted earlier, the first time we encounter Paul, he is an observer at the stoning of Stephen.

Paul evidently came from a devout Jewish home. As he writes the Philippians, he was circumcised on the eighth day, of the stock of Israel, of the tribe of Benjamin, a Hebrew of the Hebrews; as touching the law, a Pharisee; concerning zeal, persecuting the church; touching the righteousness which is in the law, blameless.[50]

In short, he would yield to no man in his dedication to the Law or in his Jewishness. Which makes it all the more ironic that this strict observer of the law should provide the most succinct statement regarding the inability of anyone to achieve righteousness by following the law. Paul writes that "not having mine own righteousness, which is of the law, but that which is through the faith of Christ, the righteousness which is of God by faith."

In other words, it is not what we do—or, as many self-righteous people would have it, what we cause others to do—that makes us righteous. In fact, we are not righteous.

When I was very young, I learned a rhyme that fits here:

There's do much good in the worst of us,

And so much bad in the best of us,

That it ill behaves any of us,

To find fault with the rest of us.[51]

---

[50] *Philippians 3:5-6*

[51] *This pithy bit of philosophy is by James Truslow Adams, an early 20th century writer and historian.*

We need to remember that there is no distance so great between us and the worst of us as there is between us and God.

The root of the problem is, I think, embodied in the name: self-righteousness. We admire our own righteousness and expect others to join in. We are missing a necessary element in approaching God in worship: humility. We forget the image of Jesus in the garden when "he fell with his face to the ground, and prayed, 'My Father, if it is thy will, may this cup be taken from me.'"[52]

In approaching essential worship, the image that we must keep in front of us is not the religious man standing proudly before God, but Christ, with his face to the ground, praying to be within the will of God.

We are told repeatedly that God lifts up the lowly and casts down the proud, but, as with so many inconvenient lessons, we skip over that and move on to something more comfortable, a rule or a law that we can keep, an act that signals our righteousness.

And we forget what God told Saul: to worship God, we must humble ourselves and pray.

---

[52] *Matthew 26:39 (NIV)*

Too Strong and Too Weak

As noted in the last two chapters, we often get in our own way when we try to draw closer to God. As with Jonah and Job, we try to define God and His purpose according to our own desires. We create a transactional relationship where we attempt to dictate the terms of the contract. And—as with the proud man praying in the public square—we claim a righteousness that we do not own, focusing on ourselves rather than God. Either of these practices is enough to keep us separated from God. Too often, we are guilty, at least to some degree, of both.

This third barrier to drawing closer to God—the one we are going to consider here—is not so straightforward. In fact, it consists of two contradictory attitudes, all stemming from a gross misunderstanding of our relationship with God.

It has to do with strength. When things are going well, we feel large and able; we feel as if we can handle everything without leaning on God.

Yet, when God calls us to meet a challenge, we come up with any number of reasons why we cannot. We, silly humans that we are, manage to both arrogate God's strength and abrogate our obedience to him. We simultaneously claim too much and too little.

The first part of this problem is largely self-correcting. I know from experience what the Bible means when it says, "Pride goeth before destruction, and a haughty spirit before a fall."[53] Unfortunately, for many of us, it is a lesson that must be frequently repeated.

The greater problem is the second part, where we use our weakness, our failings, and our humanness to try to beg off from doing God's work. God is there, His hand out, offering us the help that we've cried for, and yet, we shrink back.

I've always been puzzled at the reaction of Biblical characters to theophanies. God makes Himself visible to them in a miraculous way, and the person's response is something like, "For real?" Then, "Not me."

I believe it's because we don't understand what God wants from us when we're called. When we think about God calling us to a task, we envision ourselves as David, walking essentially unarmed onto the battlefield to fight the giant that has been placed in front of us. Instead, I think we should envision ourselves as the young Samuel, who simply replied, "Speak, for thy servant

[53] *Proverbs 16:18 (KJV)*

heareth."[54] In other words, when we hear the call of God, we shouldn't think of ourselves as the engine of the car but the wheels.

It shouldn't surprise us that we don't understand. It's an age-old truism (at least since 1763 when William Cowper wrote it) that "God works in mysterious ways, His wonders to perform."[55] And nowhere are His ways more mysterious than when He has the greatest deeds to be performed. He chose Abraham and told him to leave Ur and go to a land that he would show him. He chose Moses, a fugitive from Egypt, to rescue his people from slavery. He chose Deborah, a woman, to lead the Israelites against the army of Jabin, king of Canaan, and He chose Jael, another woman, to deal with Sisera, Jabin's general. God chose David, the youngest of Jesse's sons, to be anointed by Samuel and to lead his people. In the New Testament, Christ chose Peter, who cowered in the face of his enemies, to be the rock on which he built his church.

If God selected his heroes as we select our political candidates, probably none would have made the runoffs. However, in these choices, we find our first great lesson: God chooses whom he will, and he finds them wherever they are.

Every year at Passover, Jewish families recall their deliverance from slavery in Egypt. The ceremony

[54] *I Samuel 3:10 (KJV)*
[55] *From "Light Shining Out of the Darkness", William Cowper*

connects them to a 3500-year-old event that shaped their history. At the Seder, they ask and answer the four questions. They are homely questions, centering on why they do usual things in an unusual way: why they dip the food twice, why they eat only matzah, why they eat maror instead of any kind of vegetables, and why they all recline to eat. These things link 21st-century Jews to those who waited to be led from Egypt.

The thing that struck me is that all of these questions have an answer, recalling what the Israelites endured before they were delivered. The tears, the poverty, the bitterness of the bitter herbs, and finally the luxury of reclining like royalty to eat, because they had been saved.

I imagine that having these questions and the answers to them are comforting. However, the story has other questions which, so far as I can tell, have no answers.

Why did God choose Moses, an uncircumcised fugitive from Egyptian justice, for the task?

Why did He choose the device of the burning bush to address him?

Why did God send Moses to confront the Pharaoh and—at the same time—tell Moses that the Pharaoh would not let his people go?

And why—since God was going to use his power to convince the Pharaoh—did he need Moses at all?

These things are—to me—mysteries, more examples of God working in mysterious ways his wonders to perform.[56]

However, the story of Moses and the children of Israel shows how God uses unlikely people to do His work. This is a not-uncommon theme in the Bible, and I believe that we can draw some important lessons and an important warning from examining some of them. In this chapter, we're going to see God work in mysterious ways in two very similar stories and one that is very different.,

The story that essentially parallels God's call to Moses and His deliverance of the Israelites is Gideon, found in Judges. In both stories, God is responding to the cries of his people. And in both, he appears to the hero he has chosen. In both, the chosen hero responds with a flurry of excuses, most of which can be reduced to I'm not big enough, strong enough, or well-known enough to do what you're asking me to do.

I can identify with that. We all have reasons we cannot do what God wants us to do. We can't tithe right now because our budget is too tight or our resources too meager. We don't have time to sit with a suffering friend and comfort him. We aren't strong enough or talented enough to do the job the church has asked us to do. I am not able!

---

[56] *I am aware that there are theological theories that purport to answer each of these questions. I even have some theories. I'm also aware that I cannot fathom the mind of God, so all of these theories may be incomplete or just wrong.,*

To which God might reply, "True enough. But I am."

It's interesting to note that God is very patient with both Moses and Gideon and all of their excuses. God understands our weaknesses and insecurities. However, He's not so patient with our unwillingness. After going through all of his excuses, Moses, realizing he cannot debate with God, resorts to begging: Please send someone else. And that makes God mad. Or as Exodus 4:14 puts it: Then the Lord's anger burned against Moses.

When I was very young, I was a stubborn child. I tended to argue with my mother. Mother was a person of great, but not unlimited patience. There would come a point at which it was obvious that Mother had had as much of my smart mouth as she wanted to hear. If I was really smart, I stopped arguing. If I wasn't, my mother's anger burned against me. And I knew not to open my mouth again.

I imagine Moses felt much the same way.

The story of Gideon is to me more instructive and more entertaining than Moses and the children of Israel, perhaps because it conforms more closely to the dramatic form that I'm used to. It could be turned into a Hollywood movie without changing the structure.

When we first meet Gideon, he is in the wine-press, threshing wheat, a telling scene that immediately shows how frightened the Israelites were. The threshing floor was an open flat surface; as a part of the threshing operation, the thresher threw the wheat into the air, letting the wind blow the husks away while the seed settled to the floor. It was a labor-intensive and dusty process, and it needed a good breeze to blow the husk away. The winepress, on the other hand, was an enclosed space without a breeze to keep the air breathable or to effectively separate the wheat from the chaff. It was uncomfortable and inefficient, but to Gideon and others like him, it was a matter of trying to stay alive in what had become a hostile land.

Then the Angel of the Lord appears to Gideon, saying (in the King James version), "The Lord is with you, mighty man of valor."

Those words must have been incongruous to Gideon. Mighty man of valor? To someone hiding from his enemies? Then, "The Lord is with you." Gideon didn't believe it. First, he questions that. Then he questions why the Lord chose him.

Most of us would probably have reacted just as Gideon did, not accepting what was said, even though it was said by an angel. The problem is that we are so aware of our deficiencies that we forget that God is calling us not to be the solution, but to be His instrument.

What He wants from us is, "Speak, Lord, thy servant is listening."

Instead, He gets a litany of excuses.

Gideon wants to know why, if the Lord is with his people, the people are having such a hard time. Where are, he asks, all the miracles he's been told about? He also reminds God that he (Gideon) is the least member of the weakest clan.

Then we get into the negotiations, the test, and perhaps the strangest strategic planning session in all of history.

The first conversation between the angel and Gideon (verses 11-18)seems strangely normal considering that Gideon is talking with an emissary from God or perhaps God Himself.[57] Gideon sees irony in almost everything the angel says. He doesn't think of himself as a mighty man of valor, nor does he think that God is really with his people. They are suffering.

So Gideon asks the angel to wait while he goes to get a suitable offering. Then God consumes the offering, almost eliminating Gideon's doubts. Gideon, however, asks for several more signs, and God provides them. Then God puts Gideon to the test:

> *And it came to pass the same night, that the Lord said unto him, Take thy father's young bullock, even*

[57] *The writer of Judges seems to use "Lord" and "Angel of the Lord" interchangeably in this section. Some commentaries hold that the writer uses "Lord" when the messenger speaks with authority giving instruction, and "Angel of the Lord" in other instances. Other commentators simply write this off as being common in theophanies. Fortunately, for our purposes, it makes no difference; this is God speaking to Gideon.*

> *the second bullock of seven years old, and throw down the altar of Baal that thy father hath, and cut down the grove that is by it:*
>
> *And build an altar unto the Lord thy God upon the top of this rock, in the ordered place, and take the second bullock, and offer a burnt sacrifice with the wood of the grove which thou shalt cut down.*[58]

Gideon takes ten of his servants and does exactly as he's been told. Then comes the greater test: defeating the Midianites.

Which brings us to the second great lesson in these stories: when God calls us he equips us for his work. God sends Moses to the Pharaoh, equipping him with magic and his more eloquent brother. He equips Gideon with the number of warriors God knows he needs. He didn't tell Moses to go convince the Pharaoh by his eloquence or Gideon to use his thousands to overcome the enemy. With Moses, with Gideon, and later with David, God did not just send his chosen ones into battle. As God told Moses and Gideon, "I will be with you."

It's noteworthy that God didn't need to say the same thing to David. David already knew it. Neither did David debate with God about his wor-

[58] Judges 6:25-26 (KJV)

thiness or ability. David simply went out to fight the giant armed with his slingshot, even though his brother and the king had warned him that he wasn't up to the task.

When Goliath challenged David, David's reply was, "I come against you in the name of the Lord Almighty, the God of the armies of Israel, whom you have defied. This day the Lord will deliver you into my hands."[59]

I believe that David's attitude is a better illustration than either Moses' or Gideon's. Perhaps it's because he's a child and hasn't had time to decide that his victories depend on his own strength, or perhaps it's because the fight is so obviously unfair—a giant against a teenager. In any event, David knew that he did not face Goliath alone. He went into an impossible situation with the confidence of God's support.

In the Gideon story, God's instructions are very clear, and if you're not Gideon, they might be humorous. When Gideon sends messengers to the tribes to tribes, 32,000 potential warriors show up. Since "the Midianites and the Amalekites and all the children of the east lay along in the valley like grasshoppers for multitude, and their camels were without number," [60] Gideon probably doesn't consider 32,000 to be enough. We have already seen that Gideon follows God tentatively, even reluctantly, asking for signs of God's support,

---

[59] *1st Samuel 17: 45-46 (NIV)*
[60] *Judges 7:12 (KJV)*

then more signs. I can imagine how he must have felt when he looked across the valley at the Midianites and Amalekites, seeing that his army was badly outnumbered. He probably wanted and expected God to bring more warriors to his side.

Instead, God says:

> *"The people that are with thee are too many for me to give the Midianites into their hands, lest Israel vaunt themselves against me, saying, Mine own hand hath saved me."*[61]

Through a series of tests, God whittles Gideon's 32,000 warriors down to 300, eliminating all those who were afraid (22,000) and all those who knelt down to drink water (about 9,700). Then I can imagine God rubbing his hands together and telling Gideon that now they can go slay some Midianites and Amalekites.

It's important to note that when God gave Gideon instructions for his 300 warriors, he told them to carry a trumpet in one hand and a torch inside a pitcher in the other. That, of course, didn't leave a hand for a sword. God was showing Gideon in the clearest possible terms that victory did not depend on either Gideon's strength or the numbers of his army. It was, as noted in Deuteronomy:

---

[61] *Judges 7_12 (KJV)*

> *When you go out to battle against your enemies and see horses and chariots and people more numerous than you, do not be afraid of them; for the Lord your God, who brought you up from the land of Egypt, is with you.*[62]

Which is the third great lesson: God gives the victory. It is not that God leans on us, but that we can and must lean on God.

We all know how these stories end. Moses delivers the children of Israel from bondage in Egypt. Gideon—promoted to junior partner by God—and his 300 warriors, spook the enemy, and they run. David, of course, slays Goliath and cuts off his head. They are, in terms of the heroes' quests, happy endings.

However, we often stop reading too soon, especially in the stories of Moses and Gideon. Too often, we forget the three great lessons and ignore the warning. However, God makes it clear that, once given the victory, we are not supposed to forget who gave it to us.

In both the Moses and Gideon stories, for whatever reason, God provides the Israelites with gold; before Moses leaves Egypt, the Israelites ask the Egyptians for articles of silver, gold, and clothing, and the scripture says that the Egyptians

---

[62] *Deuteronomy 20:1-4 (NIV)*

gave the treasure to them.[63] Gideon's troops rip the rings from the ears of the Midianites.[64]

Then, in each case, something is created from the gold that becames an object of worship, supplanting their worship of the God who had brought them to that point. The Israelites in the desert made a golden calf and Gideon, having refused to rule his people, created a golden ephod, which "became a snare to Gideon and to his house."[65]

Admittedly, when I was teaching about Gideon and the power of God in defeating the Midianites, I usually stopped before I got to this part. After all, Gideon had banished the Midianites, and they didn't come back. There was peace in the land that lasted for forty years, and Gideon had many sons. It didn't sound as if God was terribly angry with him.

But again we stop reading too soon. After Gideon dies, one of his sons, Abimelech, unleashes a campaign of fratricide and bloodshed that tears the country apart. He is finally killed by his sword bearer after being disabled by a woman dropping a rock on his head.

Certainly, it's more comforting to stop reading when the good guys are winning, and God is solv-

---

[63] *Exodus 12:36 (NIV)*

[64] *Judges 8:24 There is a good deal of discussion in the commentaries about whether this refers to an earring (singular) or earrings (plural) or to nose rings. For our purposes, it makes no difference.*

[65] *Judges 8:27 (KJV)*

ing their problems. The lessons are clear. If God chooses us, we should not resist; God chooses whomever he will. If God chooses us, he will equip us, appropriately and sufficiently. And, if God chooses us, he will give us the victory, although it may not be the definition of victory that we asked for or wanted.

The Scriptures show us a sequence of events that the Israelites repeated one time after another. In their suffering, they cried to God for salvation, whether it was to be freed from slavery in Egypt, oppression by the Midianites, or any of the other disasters that befell the lad. Then, when they became comfortable again, they forgot the God who had saved them. From a thousand or two-thousand year distance, we judge them harshly, considering them to be a short-sighted and ungrateful people. But we shouldn't.

We often follow a similar pattern. Just as Gideon created the ephod and the people worship it, we have a tendency to worship our own strength, or our own intellect or our own skills. As with the Israelites in the time of Gideon, that doesn't usually work out well.

Essential worship requires the spirit of the child Samuel, who, when called by the Lord, simply said, "Speak, for thy servant listeneth."

Moving Toward Essential Worship

At the beginning this book, I made two claims for it. The first was that this book is not a scholarly work. I trust that, by now, you consider that point proved. The second claim was that it is very personal, leaning on my own experiences and—so far as my journey has gone—drawing from what I have learned.

Still, in this last chapter, I feel like a person standing just beyond the base of a mountain explaining how to get to the top, even though I have never seen the top. I haven't completed the journey, and it's probable that I never will. Still, I think I've learned some important things, and now, I will try to pass them on. This chapter will be the least scholarly and most personal of any in this book. The thoughts are, so far as I know, wholly mine, and you may disagree with them. At worst, these may prompt some thoughts of your own.

If we agree that we want to draw closer to God, to become Essential Worship, the obvious question is, "Why don't we?" In the previous chapters, we've seen how we frustrate our own efforts to close the space created at the Garden. Too often, our worship is backward. Rather than seeking God and His will, we show up with our shopping list, adult replicas of my college Sunday School student. From Job demanding an answering and answerable God to our appropriation of righteousness because we follow the rules and are probably no worse than others, we get in the way of our own relationship with God and block out our own understanding. That, too, is a lesson it's taken me many decades to acknowledge and more decades to act on.

If our own actions—our need to define our concept of God, our self-righteousness, and our reluctance to commit ourselves to doing God's bidding—are the problem, the obvious solution is to quit doing those things. It's like the old joke about the man who goes into the doctor's office and tells him that "my arm hurts when I lift it like this." Without looking up, the doctor says, "Then don't lift it like that." In other words, we may think the key to drawing closer to God is not doing the things that we know keep us separate.

Unfortunately, it is not that simple. We are human and contain an array of contradictions. We proclaim an almighty God, but we—like Job and Jonah—insist on a God defined by our needs.

We lament our sinfulness but proclaim a righteousness that we don't have. And we see ourselves as both too strong to need God and too weak to accomplish the tasks to which God calls us. The Scriptures and history are full of examples of all of these.

We see it as strange that Gideon, a man who actually saw God and triumphed following God's instructions began to worship something of his own making. The Israelites, delivered from slavery in Egypt, decided that they wanted to worship the Golden Calf. But instead of seeing that as strange, we should feel a kinship because over and over, despite great works by God in our own lives, we focus on something that we think we made—our success, our wealth, our shiny objects such as cars, jewelry, and even golf clubs.

So, how do we rid ourselves of these barriers? I believe that there are four keys that will help us get on our way. Fortunately, they are simple to explain. Unfortunately, they are difficult to practice. We'll start at the beginning.

Most of us, when we think of Psalm 46, immediately think of that comforting line at the beginning: God is our refuge and strength, a very present help in trouble. Then the psalmist goes on to say that no matter how crazy things get, we don't need to be afraid. The Psalm speaks to our fears and encourages our belief that God is more powerful than all the things that frighten us.

However, the verse that stuck with me is near the end and—while the rest of the Psalm is about God—this verse is the very voice of God.

Be still, and know that I am God.

To me, this is the first step in essential worship, and to me, it deserves a lot of thought. The commentaries I've read have been mostly unsatisfying, so I offer my own exegesis:

First, I believe that the verse is intentionally sequential: first, be still, then know.

The psalmist describes a chaotic world, one in which the waters roar, and the mountains shake and are carried into the sea. It's a world that seems much like the one we are in today. On any given day, we have thousands of thoughts, and for most of us, only a few of them are useful. Others are worries, regrets, forebodings, and other energy sinks. We have little mental capacity left for larger and more important subjects. Our world is one of reaction. First, we have to learn to be still.

When my mother told me to be still, it was usually because I was doing something that interfered with what I was supposed to be doing or something she was supposed to be doing. I think there's a direct parallel to what those words mean in the Psalm. We are, in Longfellow's words, "up and doing," but not the right things. God is working in our lives, and our doing is interfering.

I believe that "be still" means quit doing. I can no more accomplish what God can than I can still the waters' roar or the mountains' shaking. This, of course, sounds very much like meditation, a practice that some preachers have called demonic. I believe that it is obedience. If I calm my mind, then God can teach me.

If I learn to quit doing, then I can move to the second step: know that I am God. This, too, I think, means much more than we generally realize. One commentary says, "Know, in this instance, means 'to properly ascertain by seeing' and 'acknowledge, be aware.'" I don't think that this even begins to define what the psalmist means, although I will admit that I don't have a good idea what the commentator means by "properly ascertain by seeing."

Ascertain usually means to learn or confirm. It is, I think, something we do intellectually. Similarly, to acknowledge or be aware of seems shallow. I acknowledge that in my old age, my joints are more painful, and I'm certainly aware of them, but while that might change my activities, it doesn't affect my basic beliefs.

To know here means even more than the more intimate definition of "knowing" that we find in the Scriptures; it transcends both the intellectual and the physical. It penetrates us, not only into our bones but into our very marrow. In I-Thou, Martin Buber offers two important insights. In the first, he says, "The primary word (I-Thou) can only be spoken with the whole being.

He who gives himself to it may withhold nothing of himself."[66]

He goes on to say that this cannot be done "through my agency."

"To know" does not mean to study to show thyself approved. That's something else entirely. In knowing, I am not some medieval scholastic sitting for hours, puzzling over ancient manuscripts. Rather, again, I am Job, standing wordless and amazed, as God demonstrates the wonder of His creation. It is not that I learn who God is, but that His power and grandeur envelop me.

The second insight that pertains here is this: "Actually, there is no such thing as seeking God, for there is nothing in which He can't be found."[67]

So, our "knowing" is not a quest. It's not something we do so much as something we allow to be done to us. I believe that it's a matter of attitude. It is not something we grasp but something we open ourselves to. In other words, given the right attitude, God does the work. It affects important changes in me. If I really know that God is God, then I take my attention off of me and put it on God. I realize that I am not a party in a transaction but a humble being worshiping an all-powerful God. The more we know God, the more we realize how far our actions create distance from Him.

---

[66] *Buber, I-Thou, p. 10*
[67] *Buber, I-Thou, p. 80*

If in our stillness we don't hear God speaking to us, directing our thoughts, we need to listen some more. And this impacts the second thing we need to do.

In 1989, I—along with millions of others desperate to become highly effective—read Stephen Covey's book, The Seven Habits of Highly Effective People. I remember that when I read it, I thought it made a lot of sense. While I still think that it makes sense, I've come to believe that it requires careful reading and a lot of thought. As with high explosives, several of his habits can cause a great deal of damage when misused.

For instance, the first habit in the book is "Be proactive." When read casually, this probably contributed to an epidemic of "Ready-Fire-Aim" programs. However, the habit that came to mind as I was thinking about this was the second one: Begin with the end in mind.

On one level, that's unarguable. You don't usually begin a trip without knowing the destination. On a deeper level, it's as dangerous as being proactive in the wrong way. We have to make sure that we have the proper end in mind. For instance, the end that Gideon had in mind was ridding his country of its enemies and saving its people. Moses envisioned saving the Israelites from slavery in Egypt. Both of these ends were agreeable; God used Moses and Gideon to achieve them. However, both Gideon and the Israelites, after accomplishing what they thought they were trying to accomplish, turned to other gods. They had an end in mind, but not the right one.

In each case, their objective had to do with what they wanted for themselves. They wanted to be delivered from fear and from slavery. To be a nation again. It had nothing to do with bringing them closer to God.

When I pray, I find that I'm not really different from Gideon and Moses. Despite years of telling myself that I shouldn't, I still approach God with a list of things that I want: peace and security for me and my family, comfort for people I know who are suffering, guidance in decisions that I must make. There is, I think, nothing wrong with seeking God's help; however, it sometimes seems that's all we do. We need to go back to the instructions above: Be still and know that I am God.

The end that I need to keep in mind is to follow God's will, to close the space between us, and to do what God would have me do.

This last statement points to an important question: what would God have us do? There are a number of scriptures that provide some sort of answer to that question, but the one that seems the clearest and most straightforward is God's instruction to Solomon. It was mentioned earlier but is worth revisiting here.

The scene is the dedication of the temple by Solomon and the people. All the people were gathered, thousands of animals were sacrificed, and God filled the temple with his presence. Solomon prays a long prayer that says in several different ways, "When we disappoint you and realize it, let us come back to you, knowing that you will protect us." The dedication goes on for a week.

But God chooses to answer Solomon in a much quieter time, at night. God tells Solomon that He has heard his prayers and will make the temple His place. Then He tells Solomon what he expects of those who call on him.

> *If my people, who are called by my name, will humble themselves and pray and seek my face and turn from their wicked ways, then I will hear from heaven, and I will forgive their sin and will heal their land.*[68]

It seems so straightforward. If we are to claim the blessings and protection of God, then we have to recognize our perspective, our relationship with God. We don't defy God. We don't define God. And we don't hold ourselves to be righteous as God is. We are still.

---

[68] *2 Chronicles 7:14 (NIV)*

Sometimes, especially when we go beyond our external worship, we feel that we don't know how to pray, to seek God's face. Fortunately, Jesus left us with a model in the Lord's prayer, and the first half (Hallowed be thy name, Thy kingdom come, Thy will be done), is the key. It recognizes our relationship with God and the primacy of His will over ours. Essentially the Lord's Prayer repeats God's promise to Solomon: if we approach God properly—with humility and adoration—God will supply our needs and guide our actions.

Sometimes we trip ourselves up on the idea of being humble. Much of our lives depend on self-confidence and the appearance of capability. We get used to it. We are comfortable with it. Sometimes, even, we are proud of our humility. However, there's a difference in how we face the world and how we face God. We approach God knowing that He is the creator, and we are the creature, that all we have to offer is ourselves.

However, it does not mean hiding our face and crying, "I am not worthy." It is knowing—there's that word again—we are worthy, but that our worthiness comes from God and is not of our own making.

You may have noticed that to this point, everything has to do with changing how we know God and preparing ourselves. It is internal. It is our very being. These things are important, but yet it is an incomplete process. If we stopped here, we'd simply be pious hermits. There is yet another step.

I have always been fond of the book of James, mostly because it provided a clear answer to the people who considered Ephesians 2:8 (By grace are ye saved, through faith) some sort of get out of jail free card. Of course, verse 10 of that same passage tells us that we are created in Christ Jesus to do good works, but some people seem to read only the parts they want to.

The authorship of James is ambiguous, but the message isn't: faith without works is dead. Which should lead us to ask, to engage in Essential Worship, what works should we do?

It appears that we've come nearly full circle here, from our quitting doing to being commanded to do, but in that space between the two poles, we have made a major change. Our doing is no longer self-directed but is directed by God. We are not seeking our own way, but God's way for us. In our humility, we recognize that our actions are not separate from our worship but are our worship. As in I-Thou, we objectify neither the worship nor the action; they are both of the whole that is us.

I suppose that each person who truly seeks God's will experiences it personally and differently, but I believe that there are certain things that are always true. For instance, God demands our obedience. Jesus said, "If you love me, keep my commandments."[69] That's a good, if obvious, place to start, obvious because if we claim to follow Christ, we cannot ignore what he would have us do.

It was not a passing statement. Jesus was with the disciples in the Upper Room. He knew that Judas would betray him. He knew that he was leaving those who had followed him. He took the opportunity to teach them what they needed to learn to follow Him after He was gone. He washed their feet, a task typically done by a servant and told them that he was doing it as an example of what they must do.

Then He said, "A new command I give you: Love one another. As I have loved you, so you must love one another. By this, everyone will know that you are my disciples, if you love one another."[70]

Some, I suppose, would try to make an argument that Christ commands us to love those who think like us, believe like us, or look like us. However, there are a number of references that belie this interpretation, from the Parable of the Good Samaritan to Jesus' declaration that the greatest commandment is to love God and the next one—-like unto it—is to love thy neighbor as thyself. In the Parable of the Good Samaritan, Jesus expands the definition of neighbor to be without bounds and borders.

---

[69] *John 14:15 (KJV)*
[70] *John 13:34-35 (KJV)*

I personally believe that those who try to define "neighbor" with some sort of exclusivity hurt our Christian witness. The simple fact is, if we are of Christ, we love. Without definitions. Boundaries. Or qualifications. Just as he has loved us.

Useful experience comes from strange directions. For years, a part of my consulting practice was assisting corporations in developing a customer service culture. The idea was that consistent and excellent service to the customer could not be simply a matter of individual initiative, but had to be supported by the structure of the organization. We discovered that, in addition to the usual tools (e.g., accurate position descriptions, standards, etc.), one of the important elements was a simple statement that provided a measure by which employees could measure their actions. The employee's response in any customer situation would either meet the standard or not. If it didn't, something needed to change.

For instance, the "measurable standard" for one of my clients was: My job is to serve the customer so well that he won't think of going anywhere else. (I was gratified to learn this statement still decorated the walls of the client's customer service areas after forty years.)

That bit of experience was helpful when, about twenty years ago, I was pondering how to pass on some valuable grandfatherly advice to my oldest grandson. I was forever providing such advice, whether he wanted it or not. In this case, I reached back into my consulting bag and came up with what became my measurable standard. It was: I will never intentionally make anyone's life more difficult, and whenever possible, I will make it easier.

I've been told that this sounds a lot like the Golden Rule. Maybe, but I see an important difference. The Golden Rule sets me as a standard (...as I would have others do unto me). My measurable standard is an absolute, without regard to me.

It's a statement that sounds almost stupidly simple, but as I began to concentrate on practicing it, I found that it provided very understandable guidance. For instance, when someone is frustrated and out of patience and speaks sharply to me, it says that I don't respond in kind, since to do so would only increase their frustration. Or when someone pushes their buggy across my path in the grocery, I simply stop, smile, and motion for them to proceed.

Those are trivial examples. Slightly less trivial, perhaps, is my reaction to the people who are begging for money. At one time, when approached, I would go through a litany of questions in my head before responding. Is this person really trying to buy food for his family? Is he likely to use the money to support some sort of bad habit? Does he really think I'm stupid? Often, by the time I had played my question game, I would have convinced myself that the person in front of me was not worthy of my help, or—less often—that person would decide I was never going to make up my mind and wander off. The result was the same: I had lost an opportunity to make someone's life easier. Now, my decision is much less complicated; if asked for help, I give what I can. If they're conning me, that's on them.

It wasn't until I began pondering the idea (or ideal) of Essential Worship that I connected my grandfatherly impulse to my nearly lifelong quest for a closer relationship with God. I had, as so many people do, attempted to intellectualize my way to a greater discipleship, to becoming a more worthy follower. It was a humbling moment when I realized the truth: I'm just not that smart. Nor is our quest to become closer to God that complex.

Gandhi said, "The best way to find yourself is to lose yourself in service of others."[71] I think with a slight amendment that describes what I had stumbled onto. The important thing about my vow to try to make the lives of others easier was not so much what I actually did, but that my focus was no longer on me, but on others. I would amend Gandhi's statement to say that the best way to draw closer to God is to lose yourself in service of others.

---

[71] *<https://timesofindia.indiatimes.com/readersblog/civil-services-preparation/the-best-way-to-find-yourself-is-to-lose-yourself-in-service-of-others-29813/>*

It would be gratifying to say that having set my standard, I always lived up to it. It would also be untrue. I'm sure that, if they were so inclined, my family and my friends could provide lists of my failures. Fortunately, they are kinder and more forbearing than that. And I forgive myself, reminding myself that Moses only made it to the mountaintop, but he did make it to the mountaintop and did see the Promised Land.

Some years ago, the pastor at my church preached a series of sermons that provoked a lot of thought. They were on the Ten Commandments, recasting them from a prohibition to a positive action. For instance, it is not sufficient that we not kill, but—to be obedient—we must act to make lives fuller. As I got to the end of this book, I found that—in a much longer form—my journey for Essential Worship is based much on the same idea.

For two thousand years, there have been Christians who felt called upon to retreat to some sort of solitude—a monastery, a nunnery, a commune—and simply live quietly and apart with others who believed as they did. By withdrawing, they made certain that the world made little or no impact on them. What they didn't seem to consider is that they made no impact on the world either. They were like those who simply did not kill or covet or lie. I don't believe that this is how God calls us closer to Him.

Remember Job's "negative confession," all of the sins he had not committed. This, however, wasn't what reconciled him to God. It was when he stood in awe of God's creation and realized his place in it, that he responded as God would have us respond.

It's true that we must get rid of the things in our lives that distort our view of God and increase our distance. We cannot arrogate what belongs only to God and abrogate our responsibilities to Him. That is, like not murdering someone, an important but incomplete step. It is important that we seek God's will for our lives, that we are open and receptive, and without reservations. It is that as God reveals His will to us, we are listening. And once we know that will, we are acting according to it.

At the coffee shop I frequent, there's a standing joke. As I leave each time, one of the baristas will ask me what's next for me. Usually, it's just a walk or maybe a trip to the library, but my answer is always the same. "I'm off to spread cheer and joy."

And I believe that they detect a note of seriousness under the joke.

May you make progress in your journey to draw closer to God and to make your life your worship. That is Essential Worship.

www.ingramcontent.com/pod-product-compliance
Lightning Source LLC
Chambersburg PA
CBHW020412130626
46549CB00006B/2534

9798218966133